TACTICAL
PISTOL SHOOTING

Erik Lawrence

Published by

Gun Digest® Books

An imprint of F+W Publications

700 East State Street • Iola, WI 54990-0001
715-445-2214 • 888-457-2873
www.gundigestbooks.com

Our toll-free number to place an order or obtain
a free catalog is (800) 258-0929.

Library of Congress Control Number: 2004098426

ISBN-13: 978-0-89689-175-3
ISBN-10: 0-89689-175-5

Edited by Kevin Michalowski

Printed in the United States of America

DEDICATION

This book is dedicated to all those who choose to go into harm's way when called upon, especially those who are called upon when time does not allow for proper preparation for the activities to be conducted.

Train before you fight.

ACKNOWLEDGMENTS

This book could not been as easily written if not for the high-caliber and persistent individuals who constantly kicked me in the ribs to complete it. Thanks to the following individuals:

Tom Bullins of Trigger Time Valley for his expertise and guidance with dealing with left hand-dominant shooters, modern practical pistol shooting, and instructing assistance.

Jeff Cooper and Gunsite for providing me their information for the mindset chapter. Colonel Cooper has been the driving force for this subject behind many years, and many owe their lives to his work.

Chuck Jordan for assisting with all the photography and proofreading for accuracy.

Allen Martin for assisting with the initial development of the concept.

Ed Porter for applying pressure to me constantly to complete the book and proofreading.

Karen Poppele for proofing services.

Tom Wilburn, Joe Lamothe, and John Dickinson for reading and critiquing the book during development.

ABOUT THE AUTHOR

Erik Lawrence served over 10 years in the U.S. Army Special Forces, in both the 19th Special Forces Group (Airborne) and the 1st Special Forces Group (Airborne). During this time in Special Forces, Erik trained and advised numerous U.S. Military units and foreign military units in special operations training. His training and operating with some of the nation's and world's best counterterrorist units and his experience as a firearms and tactics instructor and operator for Blackheart International, LLC, have enabled him to practice and develop these techniques.

This book in some form is what the professional operators of the world are using. This is a consolidated, easy-to-read handbook that can help the layman and/or the professional operator conduct his or her training in a more organized and complete manner thus making tactical operation safer due to their competence. Whether you carry a pistol everyday in your work duties or just want to better your ability, this book will assist you in attaining the level desired.

Training Director- Blackheart International, LLC
- NRA-certified Firearms Instructor
- Monadnock Training Council Instructor
- American Heart Association Instructor
- West Virginia Law Enforcement Governor's Board Instructor
- Federal Aviation Administration Air Marshal Program Instructor
- Federal Law Enforcement Training Center- Security Specialties Division Instructor
- PPCT Management Systems, Inc., Instructor Certification
- Numerous military instructor and shooting courses
- And still operates in high threat environments requiring specialized security skills

Contents

OVERVIEW

This book's objective is to share the knowledge of pistolcraft that I have gained over the years while serving in the U.S. Army Special Forces and shooting on my personal time as well. My name is Erik Lawrence, and I have over 10 years of Special Forces experience. I am the owner of Blackheart International, L.L.C., a company formed to provide security, security training, logistics services, and other uniquely tailored services. While in Special Forces, I trained, consulted, and operated in over 30 countries with some of the host countries' elite police and military units. Since leaving the military, I have continued to travel, to operate, and to provide weapons-oriented training in Sierra Leone, Liberia, Haiti, Afghanistan and Iraq. There are no secrets to shooting well and intelligently. But it is almost impossible to learn viable pistol shooting techniques without costly professional tutors. Individuals must be on guard and avoid receiving instruction from armchair experts—those with diplomas, or no experience, and the "I could tell you but I would have to kill you" types. Remember that not all good shooters can teach you to shoot. My motive for writing this book is to share knowledge and experience and perhaps even save lives during situations that demand proper procedures for survival. I do not claim this book to be the all-inclusive bible for handgunners; it is simply another source of information for them from which to learn and facilitate progress. This book is about how to use your pistol to save your life, not fancy weapons handling.

The differences between marksmanship and combat marksmanship are truly the difference between practicing against paper and fighting for your life. Not many cases of IPSC targets attacking unsuspecting target shooters have occurred, but there are millions of cases of enemies, scumbags, and dangerous people attacking and killing others. Some of the rules must be bent to conduct effective combat marksmanship, but with proper training, they may be performed safely and quickly. This book details the use of the pistol in combat marksmanship from the basic level to more advanced life-saving techniques.

The most important point I can bring out is to receive good, sound instruction and practice, practice, and practice some more. I don't mean you should go out to the range for 12 hours and fire half million rounds; you should train efficiently and be organized. Equipment and ammunition costs are too high to waste them on unorganized training.

If one person learns one thing from this book that saves a life, then it is a success in my view. So take this book as another tool for your toolbox and never say, "I know enough".

Comments may be directed to my contact information in the back, but do not waste your time sending argumentative comments. Constructive criticism is welcomed to allow for my learning to progress also.

This book was written with the right-handed individual shooting a modern semiautomatic pistol in mind. Some techniques may transfer to the use of the revolver but should be analyzed first. Left-handed shooters should read the eleventh chapter of this book for its specific techniques and seek professional instruction.

Do not take this book lightly when it details the dirty truth about neutralizing targets. Targets are human beings, so you must accept this point before you seriously take on combat-oriented pistol shooting. Competitions are fun and organized; spur-of-the-moment close gunfights are not fun or organized. The most important thing to have in your possession at that time is the training in your head and how to apply it to the situation at hand. "Train as you fight" should be your motivation to attain your acceptable standard.

PISTOL
PROFILE

BERETTA
MODEL: PX4 STORM

Caliber	Barrel Length	Overall Length	Nom. Weight	Magazine Capacity
9mm	4 3/4"	7 3/4"	2 lbs. 4 oz.	10
40 S&W	4 3/4"	7 3/4"	2 lbs. 7 oz.	10

CHAPTER ONE

MINDSET

The use of a pistol for life-or-death encounters should be taken very seriously. Not much else is more important than saving your life and possibly taking someone else's away. You must realize this early on. Think about it. Make peace with your idea of right and wrong. Studies have shown that some people, when involved in kill-or-be-killed situations, allowed themselves to be killed rather than take the life of another. This choice is obviously a personal one, but you must prepare yourself mentally for the decision.

Col. Jeff Cooper of Gunsite, Inc., provided this chapter, and many thanks to him and his organization for this assistance. This chapter is the basis of Cooper's 1989 book, *Principles of Personal Defense*. His study of this subject continues to be the measuring device for its presentation and development. A discussion of the combat mindset is paramount to using a pistol effectively and is thus presented before we get into the mechanics of shooting.

What is MENTAL CONDITIONING?

Decent human beings have difficulty with the thought of needlessly injuring or killing another human being. We have been raised to embrace the standards of fairness, equality, kindness, gentleness and goodness toward others. Unfortunately, there are

Any type of firearms training should include a discussion of the combat mindset

many others in the world today who have no value or sense of goodness towards others.

Contrary to the exhortations of the elite, there are wolves out there– the two-legged type– and you will run across them. These individuals do not abide by laws of our government or the social standards of ethical conduct. They consider armed robbery their personal right, and your money their pay. Others in the world today believe that the religion they practice demands the exclusion of all others and even the lives of any "unbelievers." And of course, still others, who are truly and clinically emotionally disturbed, possess no sense of right or wrong. Whatever the reason, many would kill or injure you, or your family, or your friends, without remorse.

Another social reality is that the police of our society cannot protect us. Law enforcement is under no occupational obligation to do so. In fact, their job is defined as A POST-EVENT response. Investigations and the court system are a post-event system.

Department of Justice and FBI statistics estimate that one in every four adults in America will be a part of, victim of, or witness to a violent crime over the next 10 years. Interpersonal conflict is a fact of life. It is in response to this issue that many people are deciding to increase their ability for self-protection. The number of states offering concealed carry permits for citizens has grown to 45 states and one state, Vermont, allows carry with no permit at all.

Personal protection is not a new concept. This is the logical reason that many American citizens, starting from the Constitutional forefathers, have chosen to keep a firearm for self-defense. Whatever your method or plan of personal protection, you should take the responsibility to defend yourself and your family. The character trait of pro-active personal defense is not paranoia, nor is it fatalism. It provides the ability to answer more questions about life and living with increased peace of mind.

Good weapons provide an advantage, but their use requires training.

Bear in mind that if you choose to increase your ability in the area of personal defense, you must not initiate an attack. That is unlawful and immoral. However, action is always faster than reaction. If someone initiates an attack, you will have to play catch-up. The only way to increase the chances of survival is through pre-conditioning or mental conditioning. This pre-conditioning of our minds permits us to more easily defend ourselves and survive an interpersonal crisis or deadly encounter.

If you choose a firearm for personal protection, you have an obligation to perform to a significantly higher level. Carrying any weapon brings with it a higher legal, moral and ethical standard. The armed citizen must be cognizant of his surroundings; he must be able to anticipate and avoid, if possible, any potentially dangerous situations. If an armed citizen is unable to avoid a lethal confrontation, he must be able to devote his entire being to resolving the situation at hand. And, he must possess the self-control necessary to know when and how to use, or how not to use, Deadly Physical Force.

Fight like you train. A combat mindset will increase your odds of coming out alive

COMBAT TRIAD

The Combat Triad is the foundation of the doctrine taught to help students identify, assess, and respond to potential life-threatening decisions. It is composed of three elements: gunhandling, marksmanship, and mindset (mental conditioning). They may be briefly defined as the following:

GUNHANDLING: The ability to manipulate safely and responsibly the weapon/firearm. It entails presentation (deploying), loading, reloading, unloading, reducing malfunctions, and ready (responsive) positions.

MARKSMANSHIP: The ability to align firearm sights while controlling the trigger without disturbing the sight alignment.

MINDSET: Your mind is what will keep you alive in a gunfight. Your mind is your real weapon. Thus the proper mindset is paramount. The type of weapon, the caliber, or the holster in which you carry your firearm is not as important as your state of mind.

For example, gunhandling and marksmanship will allow a student to quickly get a handgun into operation for a rapid response to a threat. Anyone possessing average coordination can draw and hit a target at 7 yards in 1.5 seconds. But ... can you do it when your life is at stake and under *FIRE*? As you can see, the combat mindset is imperative.

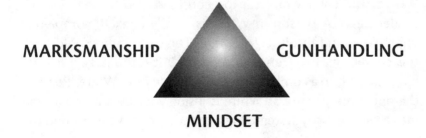

MARKSMANSHIP   GUNHANDLING

MINDSET

COMBAT MINDSET

What really is the mindset? It is a state of mind that ensures survival in a gunfight or in a life-threatening crisis. The backbone of the combat mindset is the essence of _self-control._ Certainly there is some overlap with the elements of the combat triad since dexterity and marksmanship are a prerequisite to confidence, and confidence is a prerequisite to _self-control._ However, for the _self-control_ used in the combat mindset, _awareness, anticipation,_ and _concentration_ are required.

To assist individuals in developing the awareness needed in a personal security doctrine, Col. Jeff Cooper, USMC (Ret.), modified the military alert code for civilian use. This Color Code of Awareness was started at Gunsite and is probably the single-most effective method that one can use to avoid, or counter, a life-threatening situation. Four colors keep it simple. There is no reason to add others. The colors make it easy to visualize and remember. They have nothing to do with whether or not you are armed. The Color Code helps to pre-condition your mind for the possibility of a violent attack.

Again, we do not initiate an attack. Someone else will, and we will have to play catch up. Pre-conditioning permits us to defend ourselves more easily, and survive that deadly encounter.

COLOR CODE OF AWARENESS

WHITE: The color white can be considered to be the absence of alertness. A person in White is totally relaxed, completely unprepared, and absolutely unaware of his surroundings. Pilots call this condition, "Fat, Dumb, and Happy." It is too large a mental jump to get into a combat or reactive mode from White. Possibly the only time you are at White is inside your own home as you may have a security system, dogs, and weapons in and around the home which give you delayed and planned responses. If you are attacked while in White, regardless of your ability or equipment, you may not survive.

YELLOW: Yellow is the state of mind in which one is relaxed with a nonspecific alert. There is no immediate threat, but you are alert to any possibility. In Yellow you may not be approached unaware. This increased awareness from White increases your ability to shift into a reactive or combat mode. You are not looking for trouble, but are prepared if it happens. A good example of Yellow is when you are operating your automobile. You are constantly scanning your mirrors, constantly looking for someone to do something that may cause a problem for you. Your seat belt is on, although you are not anticipating a collision. Yellow is comfortable, and you can stay in it indefinitely.

ORANGE: Orange represents a specific alert. Someone, something, or some action has attracted your attention. A crisis or violent assault may be indicated. There may be a harmless explanation to this, but you must have an answer before standing down to Yellow. It is much easier to move into your reactive or fighting mode from the awareness state of Orange than from Yellow.

RED: Red is the knowledge that "The fight is on." This is the state of mind IF your "mental trigger" or "go button" is tripped. The mental trigger may be a firearm pointed at you, a man rapidly approaching you with an upraised bat or advancing toward you with a knife, or any other gesture that you have pre-determined to be potentially life threatening. The mental trigger may depend on a variety of circumstances, but the decision to use deadly physical force has been made. It may not result in your having to use this force, but the decision has already been made by you. If they do "that," you will do "this." From Red, you will not have to play "catch-up" mentally. You are ready.

With the color code, you do not have to move up (or down) the list sequentially. You can jump from Yellow to Red, bypassing Orange. But, White has been shown to have too long a dwell time for response to critical situations. Once you begin practicing and increasing your awareness with the color code, other elements of mental conditioning will help you determine how your reaction should be employed for crisis intervention. These elements are called the principles of self-defense.

*A good gun is nothing
without a good plan*

PRINCIPLES OF SELF-DEFENSE

Alertness:

◆ Be aware of all that is around you.

◆ Know what is behind you (remember 360° security).

◆ Pay particular attention to anything that is out of place. (What's wrong with this picture?)

◆ Trust your instinct. Your stomach has no ego. If it is queasy, there is probably a reason for it.

◆ Set your mental condition to Yellow. Don't get caught in White.

Decisiveness:

◆ Select a correct course of action and carry it through without hesitation or deviation.

◆ He who hesitates is indeed lost.

◇ *"A simple plan, well rehearsed and violently executed, offers the best chance for success."* (*Ranger Handbook* as per Ranger Wilburn)

Aggressiveness:

◆ We do not initiate, but thereafter should return the attention with what should be overwhelming violence.

◆ Your response if attacked should not be fear, but anger. Fear can be changed into anger. Do it. They should NOT have the right to do that! They will not have the right!

Speed:

◆ Speed is the key absolute in any form of effective combat.

◆ The perfect fight is over before the loser really understands what is going on.

◇ *"I may lose a battle, but I will never lose a minute."* (Napoleon)

Coolness (and if firearms are used, Precision):

◆ Controlled anger is no obstacle to efficiency.

◆ If you know that you can keep your head, and know that you **must** keep your head, you probably will keep your head.

Ruthlessness:

◆ The attack must be stopped. **Do not hold back**.

◆ Your first concern is to stay alive.

◆ Strike no more after he is incapable of action, but see that he is **stopped**!

◇ **"Never, never, never give up."** (Winston Churchill)

Surprise:

◆ Surprise is the first principle of offensive combat.

◆ Do what your assailant least expects you to do.

◆ Achieve tactical surprise. The criminal does not expect you to fight back. May he never choose you, but if he does, surprise *him*.

Probably the most common question about the principles of personal defense relates to fear. Fear is one of man's greatest motivators. How do we examine fear and make it work for us?

Fear:

Fear is said to have three components. They are:

◆ Cognitive: Which is an anticipatory anxiety—a sixth sense.

◆ Physiological: From our body's chemical cocktail of adrenaline.

◆ Overt behavior: The manifestation of our actions.

Learn that fear takes time to build. It is physiologically and psychologically similar to anger. Anger is the proper antidote to fear. How? Gain the knowledge of your mind and body's stress responses. Recognize them and learn what you can do to direct those physiological actions.

Psychologists call this a "startle response.":

- ◆ If caught unaware, the head will crunch down into shoulders. Some may "freeze." You can train out of this.

- ◆ Chemical Cocktail- Adrenaline, cortisol, and dopamine are released into your system. These cause blood to be diverted from skin, extremities, and digestive organs to the large muscle groups related to speed and strength. (This is the "fight or flight" response.)

- ◆ Nausea is caused as a portion of the blood supply from the stomach is shifted to large muscle groups.

- ◆ The heart/lungs work harder and faster. The rhythm and volume are increased. Tachycardia- the heart rate doubles. Breathing increases.

- ◆ The blood pressure increases in response to the heart and adrenaline (another reason to stay in shape).

- ◆ Spleen discharges additional red blood cells to increase the oxygen supply.

- ◆ Sweat glands kick in to increase body cooling.

- ◆ General muscle groups tighten, limiting mobility.

- ◆ Extra blood is made available for large muscle groups, providing less blood for small muscle groups, resulting in less dexterity. (This point is why we emphasize gross motor skills.)

- ◆ Salivary glands shut down. Dry mouth occurs.

- ◆ Auditory exclusion- Both physical and physiological. Gunshots and other sounds may not be clearly heard.

- ◆ Tunnel Vision- Eyes dilate. Focus may be on opponent's weapon, but other objects blur.

- ◆ Visual Slowdown- Things may appear to be happening in slow motion.

- ◆ Time- Spatial distortion.

- ◆ Denial- "Is this really happening to me?" Some may be stuck here. If this is the case, you will lose.

- ◆ Altered decision process.

How can one manage these effects?
SURVIVAL STRESS MANAGEMENT

The elements of survival stress management are:

◆ Immediately slow your breathing (tactical breathing).
◆ Prioritize the threats. (How do we eat an elephant? One plate at a time.)
◆ Visualize what needs to be done to stop the attack.
◆ Take the proper course of action.

Studies indicate that certain types may be pre-disposed to survive life-threatening situations. These types include, but are not limited to:

◆ Aggressive personalities
◆ Pre-conditioned individuals
◆ Those who have survived similar situations in the past

In order to survive, you must first accept that this can, and may, happen to you. You must be prepared to deal with this type of situation, at any time. You cannot make an appointment for an emergency; you must deal with it NOW!

◆ Meet the threat. Accept that it is there. This can happen to me!
◆ Everything fits into the operational concept. Fit it in yours.
◆ Develop a street-smart mindset.
◆ Your attitude should be composed of self-control and concentration.
◆ The excitement won't kill you, but surprise will.
◆ Don't get locked into stereotypes. The threat may be male or female, young or old, Black, White, Hispanic, Asian, or whatever. Be alert.
◆ Above all, you must have the confidence and ability to win. The Combat Triad. Watch your front sight, and control the trigger straight to the rear.

Let's put all this information into a large picture frame and organize the aspects of the color code, the principles of defense, pistolcraft, mental awareness, and mindset. A good picture of this portrait might look like this outline for developing a personal security doctrine.

DEVELOP A PERSONAL SECURITY DOCTRINE

A personal security doctrine is key to establishing effective pro-active personal protection.

These are the "Keys" to Threat Avoidance:

◆ A street-smart mindset

◆ Threat analysis

◆ Tradecraft

1. STREET-SMART MINDSET

Mental Preparation:

◆ Defeatism will defeat...YOU!

◆ Even if you are forced to give up, don't give in.

◆ Accept responsibility for your actions. What you do in a heartbeat will be reviewed by many others over a long period of time. Deal with it.

◆ Don't be a victim. Don't look like prey.

Mental Conditioning:

◆ Your mind is like your body. It must be conditioned to respond.

◆ You have to build on your training. The skills are perishable, and the training must be continuous. Stay current!

◆ In a life-threatening situation, you will not rise to the occasion; you will simply default to your level of training.

Mental Awareness:

◆ Color codes

◆ Simulations ... Practice the "What if?"

2. THREAT ANALYSIS

Situational awareness: What is the nature of the threat? Home invasion, street robbery, car jacking, larceny from or of auto, etc.

◆ Time of day: Violent crimes are more likely to occur after dark.

◆ Public events or significant social anniversaries

◆ Geography: High-crime neighborhoods, locations, places

3. TRADECRAFT

Training of self-defense tools (standard/improvised), distance, and movement. Distance is your friend. Get the best and most training you can.

◆ Alter routes to bypass hazardous areas

◆ Surveillance detection

◆ All aspects of threat avoidance are intertwined

◆ Avoid dangerous situations, every time you can

If you cannot avoid danger, do whatever you must to stay alive.

Be prepared–not paranoid.

Once trained, visually rehearse different situations. Many training courses use this visualization to allow for practice wherever you are. This allows you to be quicker at deciding what course of action you are going to execute. It is free, no one can stop you from doing it at any time, and you decide what the situation will be. Once trained, you will be able to make timely, intelligent decisions to solve problems.

PISTOL
PROFILE

MADE IN USA

BROWNING® PRO-9

BROWNING
MODEL: PRO-9

Caliber	Barrel Length	Overall Length	Nom. Weight	Magazine Capacity
9mm	4 "	7 1/4"	1 lbs. 14 oz.	10
40 S&W	4 "	7 1/4"	2 lbs. 1 oz.	10

CHAPTER TWO

PISTOL NOMENCLATURE & TERMS

+P- Ammunition that is loaded to higher pressures than standard ammunition. Typical examples include: 9mm+P and .38 Special +P

+P+- Ammunition loaded to even higher pressures than +P ammunition.

ACTION- The series of moving parts that allow a pistol to be loaded, fired, and unloaded.

AUTOLOADER- A pistol that automatically reloads itself as long as it has rounds in its magazine.

BACKSTRAP- Rear, vertical portion of the pistol frame between the grip panels.

BARREL- The metal tube through which a projectile passes on its way to the target; contains the riflings that produce the spin for stable flight of the bullet.

BORE- The inside of the barrel.

BREAK OF THE SHOT- The instant the weapon fires.

CALIBER- Diameter of the bullet and the distance between the lands and grooves of the bore.

CARTRIDGE- Ammunition completely assembled with the projectile, powder, case, and primer.

CENTERFIRE- Cartridge with the primer centered in the base of the case.

CHAMBER- The rear part of a barrel in which a cartridge is contained when it is loaded and fired.

CLIP- Metal device that holds loaded rounds and assists loading into a magazine; most call magazines "clips," but they are quite different in their appearance and their uses.

CONCEALMENT- Anything that hides you from view, but does not provide enough protection to stop bullets.

CONTROLLED PAIR- Two well-aimed shots that have three distinct sight pictures (one before the first shot and one after each shot); the second shot should be delivered as soon as the pistol has settled enough to reacquire the correct sight picture and sight alignment. Used when the distance or size of the target requires a very accurate shot.

COVER- A barrier that will stop bullets and thus protect you from being shot.

CROSS-EYE DOMINANT- When a shooter's dominant side is different than his dominant eye. Example: a right-handed person is left-eye dominant.

CYCLE OF OPERATION- The functions of the pistol during firing. Feeding, chambering, locking, firing, unlocking, extracting, ejecting, and cocking.

DECOCKING LEVER- The mechanical part of the pistol that allows the shooter to safely lower the hammer on a cocked pistol. Most double-action pistols are built with one for safety.

DISCRIMINATING FIRE- Shooting engagements that are conducted with both good and hostile targets in the same area. Shots must be taken only at the hostile targets, with no collateral damage to the friendly targets.

DOUBLE-ACTION- A pistol that both cocks and releases the hammer or internal firing mechanism when the trigger is pulled.

DOUBLE-FEED MALFUNCTION, TYPE III- See failure-to-extract malfunction.

DOUBLE TAP- A type of engagement that places two rapidly fired shots consecutively onto a single target. Flash sight pictures are acquired to speed up the engagement. The distance and size of the target greatly determine whether you use a controlled pair or a double tap-type engagement.

DRY FIRING- The act of practicing with your equipment and pistol without using ammunition. You can use dummy weapons, ammunition, and/or magazines.

EJECTOR- The pistol part that ejects the empty casing or cartridge from the pistol.

FAILURE-TO-FIRE MALFUNCTION, TYPE I- This malfunction is created by the operator's attempt to fire on an empty chamber or a defective round, which will not fire. Refer to Chapter Seven.

Failure-to-extract malfunction, Type III- This malfunction (sometimes called the "double feed") is created when the fired casing in the chamber is not extracted from the chamber and the next round is rammed behind it in the pistol's attempt to feed the next round. Refer to Chapter Seven.

Failure-to-eject malfunction, Type II- This malfunction (sometimes called the "stovepipe") is created when the spent casing is not fully ejected from the weapon during firing. Typically they are vertical or horizontal stovepipe malfunctions that are created when the casing is caught by the return of the slide to chamber the next round. Refer to Chapter Seven.

Firing foot- The strong-side foot. For the right-handed shooter, it is the right foot and opposite for the left-handed shooter.

Firing pin- The mechanical part of the pistol that strikes the primer on the round when the hammer is released.

Flash sight picture- Using the front sight only to engage targets quickly . You may also superimpose the rear profile of the pistol onto the target to speed up the engagement. This technique must be practiced as it is less accurate if not conducted correctly. The distance and size of the target greatly influence the use of a flash sight picture.

Frame- The main part of the pistol that is the building block on which all other parts are attached.

Front Strap- The front of the pistol's grip that is below the trigger guard.

Grip- The handle part of the pistol you grasp; also the term for the way you hold the pistol with your hands.

HAMMERS- The firing of two very rapid shots with only one sight picture; your target is large and is close enough to hit during recoil from the first round.

HANGFIRE- A noticeable delay in the ignition of a cartridge after the primer has been struck by the firing pin.

HIGH-READY POSITION- A resting position with a two-handed grip on the pistol and the muzzle oriented 45 degrees into the air. This position is unsafe in my view and is not taught. When this is practiced on the range and then applied to tactical operations, it makes the chance of an accidental discharge into someone's head too likely (close proximity to team members and high stress can equal an avoidable disaster). It is now popular to call step three of the draw and presentation the high ready; this is semantics.

KNEELING POSITION- This shooting position is used when you need to utilize low cover or a lower, steadier position from which to shoot—very useful when shooting while wounded. Refer to Chapter Five.

LOW-READY POSITION- A shooting position that is utilized to rest in between drills or while waiting for a situation to change. Refer to Chapter Five.

MAGAZINE- A storage device designed to hold rounds ready for insertion into the chamber.

MAGAZINE RELEASE- The mechanical device that allows you to remove the magazine that is locked in the magazine well. On pistols, this is usually a button.

MAGAZINE SPRING- The spring in the magazine that forces the loaded rounds to the top of the magazine.

MALFUNCTION- Anytime a weapon fails to operate. There are three types of malfunctions that we will deal with: failure-to-fire-Type I, stovepipe-Type II, and double feed-Type III. Refer to Chapter Seven.

MISFIRE- A cartridge that failed to fire when the primer was struck by the firing pin.

MOZAMBIQUE DRILLS- This drill is a type of failure-to-stop drill. When the target is not neutralized by normal target engagement techniques, this method is used to ensure neutralization. At least two shots are fired to the center of mass (the chest); then at least one round is fired at the upper center of mass (the head).

MUZZLE- The front end of the barrel from which the bullet exits.

MUZZLE FLASH- The amount of flash produced when you fire your pistol. The barrel length, type of powder, and powder charge, along with the atmospheric conditions and ambient light level, determine the brightness of the flash.

NON-FIRING FOOT- The weak-side foot. For the left-handed shooter, it is the right foot and opposite for the right-handed shooter.

PIE OFF- Movement technique to look around visual barriers incrementally; also called the seven-meter side step.

PISTOL- An autoloading firearm that has a short barrel and can be held, aimed, and fired with one hand. A revolver uses a rotating cylinder, typically with six chambers. A pistol is magazine-fed.

POSITION FOUR- The fourth step in the presentation of the pistol. Refer to Chapter Five.

POSITION ONE- The first step in the presentation of the pistol. Refer to Chapter Five.

POSITION THREE- The third step in the presentation of the pistol. Refer to Chapter Five.

POSITION TWO- The second step in the presentation of the pistol. Refer to Chapter Five.

PRESENTATION- The movement from position three to position four. This motion is straight toward the target like on a rail system so engagements may be conducted if needed before you are at full presentation.

PRESS CHECK- The act of insuring that your chamber is loaded after you load your pistol. With your finger off the trigger, pull the slide slightly to the rear and see the brass of the casing being pulled from the chamber. At night you will have to feel for the casing to ensure it is there.

PRONE POSITION- The position taken when lying on the ground. Refer to Chapter Five.

READY POSITION- The tactical resting position that is identical to position three of the presentation. Key points to this position are that the pistol is ready for use under the dominant eye and the front sight is visible with the peripheral vision.

RECOIL SPRING- The spring in the pistol that returns the slide forward after the pistol has fired.

RHYTHM DRILL- This drill is used to develop a smooth rhythm, speed, accuracy, and the proper follow-through and recovery.

ROUND- Another word for cartridge.

SAFETY CATCH- Also called the safety. The mechanical device designed to reduce the chance of accidental discharges. Most disengage or block the firing pin when engaged.

SEMI-AUTOMATIC- A pistol which fires a single round each time the trigger is pulled, extracts and ejects the empty case, and inserts a new round into the chamber.

SHOOTING WHILE WOUNDED- The act of shooting while only using one arm because the other is injured.

SIGHTS- Mechanical, optical, or electronic devices used to aim firearms.

SIMUNITIONS FX- Brand of training ammunition that uses a non-lethal pellet filled with colored soap for marking of shots.

SINGLE-ACTION- A pistol action type that only releases the hammer when the trigger is pulled.

SLIDE LOCK- When your pistol is shot until it is empty and the empty magazine locks the slide to the rear.

SLIDE RELEASE- Mechanical part of your pistol that is used to lock your slide to the rear when the magazine is empty. Release the slide from slide lock by pushing straight down on the slide release.

SLIDE- The moving part of the pistol on top of the action that removes a round from the magazine and inserts it into the chamber. The extractor on the slide pulls the round from the chamber, and it is then ejected from the pistol as the slide is forced to the rear.

SLINGSHOT- A slang term for a technique of closing a locked-to-the-rear slide. The slide is gripped at the rear serrations with your non-firing thumb and index finger and pulled to the rear, then this grip is released to allow it to return forward by its own spring tension. If you use the "slingshot" technique, pivot the pistol on the bore (right-handed shooters pivot the slide to the left) to have the slide meet your non-firing hand. Grasp the rear serrations of the slide, pull the slide slightly rearward, and release. Regrip into your two-handed grip as you roll your sights back up and present back to the threat.

SLOW-AIMED FIRE- Deliberate slow fire using sights when great accuracy is needed and time is available.

SPEED RELOAD- The speed reload is used when you have shot all the rounds in your pistol and your slide is locked to the rear. Refer to Chapter Six.

SQUIB- A round which develops less than normal pressure or velocity after ignition and sometimes does not leave the barrel after a soft "pop."

STANDING POSITION- This position is the most common shooting platform and is detailed in Chapter Five.

STOVEPIPE MALFUNCTION, TYPE II- See failure-to-eject malfunction.

STRONG-HAND SHOOTING- This position is used to fire your pistol with only the strong shooting hand. It may be used when you are shooting while wounded or while holding something that is obviously more important than your steady two-hand shooting grip. Refer to Chapter Nine.

SUPPORTED POSITION- The use of an object to steady your shooting position. Refer to Chapter Five.

TACTICAL RELOAD- The tactical reload is used to reload your pistol with a fully loaded or almost fully loaded magazine before you move or anticipate a renewed assault on your position. It is controlled so you will maintain control of the magazines, the one being replaced and the one replacing it. Refer to Chapter Six.

TARGET FIXATION- Watching a target for a reaction when you should be analyzing or scanning to see if other threats are present.

TARGET INDEXING- The moving of your pistol from target to target. Multiple targets require some thought as how to engage in a prioritized order. Avoid target fixation or watching a target for a reaction when you should be engaging another target.

TRIGGER GUARD- Located on the underside of the frame, protecting the trigger from accidental discharges.

TRIGGER- The trigger is located on the lower part of the frame. When the trigger is pulled, it activates the hammer or the internal firing mechanism which, when released, causes the firing pin to strike and fire the round.

WEAK-HAND SHOOTING- This position is used to fire your pistol with only the weak non-shooting hand. It may be used when you are shooting while wounded or practicing the same. Refer to Chapter Nine.

WEAPON RETENTION POSITION- This position is used when you encounter an immediate threat within three feet and the threat is offensive. Refer to Chapter Eight.

SINGLE-ACTION PISTOL NOMENCLATURE

1. Slide	8. Takedown pin	15. Ejection port
2. Slide release	9. Backstrap	16. Magazine release
3. Frame	10. Front strap	button
4. Grip safety	11. Grip panel	17. Magaine well
5. Trigger	12. Hammer	18. Muzzle
6. Safety	13. Rear sight	
7. Trigger guard	14. Front sight	

DOUBLE-ACTION/SINGLE-ACTION PISTOL NOMENCLATURE

1. Slide
2. Slide release
3. Frame
4. Decocker lever
5. Trigger
6. Takedown lever
7. Trigger guard
8. Backstrap
9. Front strap
10. Grip panel
11. Hammer
12. Rear sight
13. Front sight
14. Ejection port
15. Magazine release button
16. Magaine well
17. Muzzle

GLOCK SAFE-ACTION PISTOL NOMENCLATURE

1. Slide
2. Slide stop
3. Trigger safety
4. Frame
5. Trigger
6. Trigger guard
7. Backstrap
8. Front strap
9. Grip panel
10. Takedown lever
11. Rear sight
12. Front sight
13. Ejection port
14. Magazine release button
15. Accessory rail
16. Magazine
17. Muzzle

CYCLE OF OPERATION EXPLAINED
FOR A SEMIAUTOMATIC PISTOL

Most semiautomatic pistols follow these steps for operation, and this is only included to refresh some memories.

FEEDING- The placing or a loaded round in the path of the slide.

CHAMBERING- The moving of the round from the magazine to the chamber.

LOCKING- The sealing of the round in the chamber, then locking the breach end of the barrel into the slide.

FIRING- The ignition of the primer by the firing pin thus firing the round.

UNLOCKING- The unsealing of the breach end of the barrel and unlocking the barrel from the slide.

EXTRACTING- The pulling of the spent casing out of the chamber (where a double-feed malfunction can occur due to broken cartridge rim or broken extractor).

EJECTING- The pushing of the spent casing out of the ejection port (where a stovepipe malfunction can occur if the slide is retarded in its cycling).

COCKING- The returning of the firing mechanism to the cocked and ready-to-fire position.

NOTE: Some pistols are obviously different as single-action, double-action, double-action-only, and safe-action, so educate yourself on your pistol and know how the cycle of operation works on it.

TAURUS
MODEL: PT99

Caliber	Barrel Length	Overall Length	Nom. Weight	Magazine Capacity
9mm	5"	8 1/2"	2 lbs. 2 oz.	17+1

CHAPTER THREE

SAFETY CONCERNS

When dealing with weapons, safety can never be forgotten. The more professionally an individual deals with his weapon and applies constant safety considerations, the more he shows his competence to others. Reckless handling of your weapon and the lack of regard for what weapons are capable of doing quickly show when you are being observed on the range. This observation is another you must make when you are maintaining your situational awareness. If you cannot safely handle your weapons, chances are you are just as inept at firing them. You must also take the responsibility for proper storage of weapons and their ammunition. Gun vaults, cable locks and trigger locks should be used when the situation dictates. Read and understand your manufacturer's operation and safety manual that came with your weapon.

The primary safety on any weapon is not the mechanical one; it is your brain attached to your shooting index finger, which will be resting along the pistol's frame until it is placed on the trigger when you decide to shoot. The finger is placed on the frame so there is less of a chance of an accidental discharge of the weapon. An accidental discharge may be caused by a reactive clinching of the muscles when you are surprised. This can happen if your finger is on the trigger or trigger guard. It can't if your finger is on the frame.

The following safety considerations are suggestions. You should use some or all of them when the situation dictates. Always use common sense when handling firearms, and do not sacrifice quality training because it is too dangerous to the eyes of the untrained.

1. WEAPON SAFETY

A. Treat all weapons as if they were loaded, even if you have made sure they are unloaded.

B. Keep your finger off the trigger and out of the trigger guard until on target with intention to shoot.

C. Never let your muzzle cover anything you are not willing to destroy.

D. Be sure of your target and consider its background.

E. Do not handle weapons within eight hours of consuming alcohol, drugs, or medication that may impair judgment or the ability to handle a weapon safely.

F. Decock or engage the safety on your weapon when not on target or when told to do so by someone of authority.

NOTE: When using the double-action pistols, I teach students to decock them and leave their safety in the fire position because they are using the trigger finger as the primary safety, allowing them to smooth out their draw. It is a safe method when practiced and rule "B" listed above is not violated. For single-action weapons, the safety is on until they are oriented towards the threat in their shooting sequence. After engagements, the trigger finger comes off the trigger, the double-action is decocked, and the decocker is returned to the fire position. The single-action is put back on safe. It is essential to practice each time in order for it to become a reflex.

2. FIRING LINE- (FLAT RANGE)

A. Keep the pistol holstered, except when on the firing line or told to do otherwise by the instructors.

B. Stay in line with other shooters.

C. Never turn around with a pistol in your hand. Holster it first, then turn.

D. Never dangle a pistol in one hand.

E. Always use eye and ear protection.

F. Take your finger off the trigger and out of the trigger guard when moving off target.

G. Never shoot a target up range (opposite the direction of fire) or outside of designated range boundaries.

H. Use the designated weapon repair area to correct weapon deficiencies.

I. Do not load until told to do so.

3. RANGE PROCEDURES

A. Always have some form of medical bag and know its location while you are at the range.

B. Know the location of a cellular phone with the emergency numbers preprogrammed and a fill-in-the-blank form to include the who, what, when, and where information the EMS operator will require when assisting you.

C. The primary instructor clears weapons when leaving the range for the day.

D. Pay attention to other shooters and use common sense with range etiquette.

E. Never move down range without clearance from other shooters.

F. Do not shoot objects not designated as targets.

G. Shooters will clear malfunctions if possible. If not, call for the primary instructor.

H. Keep your finger off the trigger while conducting reloads and malfunction correction drills.

I. Anyone can call a cease fire if they see an unsafe act.

4. RANGE COMMANDS

A. "Load and make ready."

1) Lock the slide to the rear.

2) Place the magazine in the weapon.

3) Chamber a round.

4) Press check and decock or engage the safety.

LOADING YOUR PISTOL

FIGURE 3-1

STEP ONE- Lock the slide to the rear by pulling the slide to the rear and pressing up on with the slide release. Once it is engaged, release the slide tension.

FIGURE 3-2

FIGURE 3-3

STEP TWO- With the pistol pointed in a safe direction, insert the loaded magazine into the magazine well refer to Figure 3-2. Fully seat the magazine with the heel of the hand to ensure it is locked in by the magazine release refer to Figure 3-3. Your palm should be hard, as your fingers should be extended, not relaxed.

NOTE: Note the shooter is keeping the pistol close to his body, which provides him much more dexterity than with his arms extended or at his waistline. Index your elbows on your ribcage to maintain consistency in your actions. Think "eye, muzzle, target" to keep the correct alignment to save time on the re-engagement. Think of where you thread a needle, and this is about where you need to perform reloads and malfunction corrections. Some call it the 16-inch circle theory as per Jason Mook.

FIGURE 3-4

FIGURE 3-5

STEP THREE- With single-action pistols, you must pull the slide (by gripping the serration on the rear of the slide, not over the ejection port) to the rear and release it to slam shut by *its own spring tension refer to Figure 3-4.* Return the pistol's safety catch to the safe position. An alternative method is to press down on the slide release and allow it to shut by its *own spring tension refer to Figure 3-5.* Return the pistol's safety catch to the safe position. Ensure the slide is in battery (fully forward).

With double-action pistols, you can pull the slide to the rear while the pistol's safety is engaged and release it to slam shut by *its own spring tension* or press down on the slide release and allow it to shut by *its own spring tension*. Ensure the slide is in battery (fully forward).

STEP FOUR- Perform a press check to guarantee your chamber is loaded. Figures 3-6, 3-7, and 3-8 are three techniques to perform a safe press check; ensure your finger is off the trigger. To perform a press check on a single-action pistol, you must disengage the safety catch, pull the slide back slightly so you may see the brass of the casing showing, release the slide, and place the pistol back on safe. Do not pull the slide back too far because

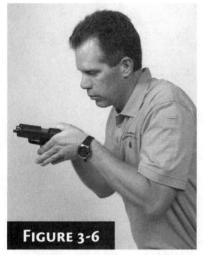

FIGURE 3-6

FIGURE 3-7

this action will make the pistol eject the loaded round. On the double-action pistol, you do not have to disengage the safety catch, so you just have to pull the slide slightly to the rear and see the brass casing refer to a Figure 3-8. Some of the newer pistols have a loaded chamber indicator; see your pistol manufacturer's instruction booklet. If there is a lot of tension on the slide, you may have to cock the

FIGURE 3-8

hammer to press check, then decock if needed. At night you will have to feel the casing with a non-firing finger.

B. "MAKE WEAPON SAFE."

1) Decock, holster, or engage the safety of the pistol, and point it in a safe direction.

This could be a command to reholster also.

C. "CLEAR YOUR WEAPON."

1) Engage the safety. Utilize the particular safety your weapon has and remove the magazine while the muzzle is oriented in a safe direction.

2) Pull the slide to the rear and lock it with the slide release. Allow the round to fly out–observe round being ejected; do not try to catch it. Pick it up once you have successfully cleared your weapon.

3) Inspect the empty magazine well (see the ground through the magazine well).

4) Inspect for an empty chamber—**TWICE!**

5) Release slide without allowing it to slam shut by its own spring tension.

6) Safe, holster, and/or case weapon.

CLEARING/UNLOADING YOUR PISTOL

FIGURE 3-9

STEP ONE- Remove the magazine; put the pistol on safe refer to Figure 3-9.

STEP TWO- Pull the slide to the rear and lock it with the slide release refer to Figure 3-10. Allow the round to fly out–observe round being ejected; do not try to catch it. Pick it up once you have successfully cleared your weapon.

FIGURE 3-10

FIGURE 3-11

STEP THREE- Inspect the empty magazine well (see the ground through the magazine well). Refer to Figure 3-11.

STEP FOUR- Inspect the chamber–**TWICE!** In low-light situations, you may *physically* have to feel into the chamber with your pinkie finger refer to Figure 3-12.

FIGURE 3-12

STEP FIVE- Release slide without allowing it to slam shut by its own spring tension refer to Figure 3-13.

STEP SIX- Place the pistol on safe, then holster and/or case weapon.

FIGURE 3-13

PISTOL PROFILE

SPRINGFIELD

MODELS: XD9401HC
XD9402HC
XD9403HC

Caliber	Barrel Length	Overall Length	Nom. Weight	Magazine Capacity
9X19mm	5.01 "	8 "	1 lbs. 15 oz.	15
.40 S&W	5.01 "	8 "	1 lbs. 15 oz.	12
.357 SIG	5.01 "	8 "	1 lbs. 15 oz.	12

CHAPTER FOUR

SHOOTING FUNDAMENTALS

Before we start learning the basic shooting fundamentals, we must determine the shooter's dominant eye.

1. **Dominant eye:** The definition of the dominant eye is the eye that you use primarily to see details, with the assistance of the less-dominant eye. The shooter should always aim with his dominant eye. If the shooter is right-handed and cross-eye dominant, the shooter just orients the pistol under the left (dominant) eye at position three to four during presentation. To find out which eye is dominant, take this simple foolproof test.

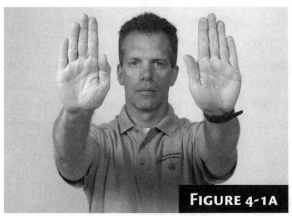

Eye Dominance Test Step 1

FIGURE 4-1A

*Eye Dominance
Test Step 2*

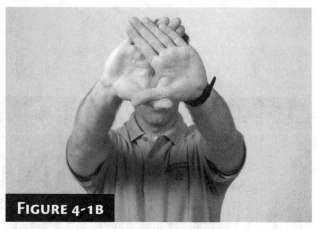

FIGURE 4-1B

*Eye Dominance
Test Step 3*

FIGURE 4-1C

A. Extend both arms in front of your body refer to Figure 4-1A.

B. Place the hands together, forming a small opening between them refer to Figure 4-1B.

C. With both eyes open, look at a distant object through the opening that was formed.

D. Keeping focused on the distant object, bring your hands back to your face. Bring them back until they touch your face refer to Figure 4-1C.

E. The eye that the opening is over is your dominant eye. If you have doubt, repeat the steps to be sure of your dominant eye.

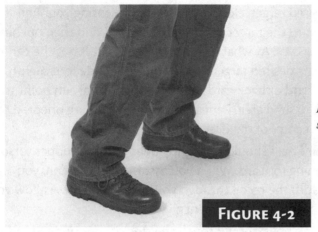

*Fighter's
stance*

FIGURE 4-2

2. **Stance:** This fundamental of shooting is always important; it is the foundation for your shooting platform. For combat-type shooting, the stance should be solid, yet potently ready for movement. This stance looks like a fist fighter's stance. This stance should be very similar to your shooting stance for tactical carbines and shotguns and with the empty-hand martial arts. The less you have to change for different weapon systems, the more natural it will be. Make this stance a habit.

A. The feet should be shoulder-width apart. The non-firing foot is slightly forward of the firing foot (usually 3-6 inches) and is pointed to the target to be engaged. Your firing foot should be firmly planted and at up to a 45-degree angle outboard to provide you with balance. Weight distribution between the non-firing foot and firing foot should be 60/40 and focused on your toes (essential in recoil management). Refer to Figure 4-2. Your weight should be centered over the balls of your feet. This position also allows for quick lateral or forward movement. Natural point of aim is very important for beginning shooters, as it is where the body naturally points and is a good starting place so you are not correcting for other mistakes. You can find your natural point of aim by acquiring your stance oriented at the desired target, closing your eyes, presenting your hands toward the target as if holding a pistol, and then opening your eyes. At what are you oriented? If it is not the center of the desired target, move your firing side foot slightly forward or backward to bring your natural aim point to the desired area. Repeat until your hands are oriented to the center of the desired target.

B. Your knees should be slightly bent and your upper torso leaning forward. When you assume this position, you absorb the recoil through your body, which will allow you to speed up engagements.

C. Your elbows should touch the side of your body. Stand with your head and shoulders square to the target and your head erect.

D. <u>Your stance must be comfortable, so make sure you attain it every time you start your practice</u>, refer to Figure 4-3. It is quick to move from, you present your stongest part of your body armor, if used, and you are facing the known threat so you can analyze your courses of actions with the most amount of information available.

Relaxed stance

FIGURE 4-3

3. **Grip:** This section will teach a right-handed shooter that is right-eye dominant.

A. With your weapon pointed in a safe direction and the index finger off the trigger and outside the trigger guard, use the non-firing hand to place the pistol in the web of the shooting hand. Make a fist around the handle of the pistol. Your grip should allow you to place your trigger finger so that you have maximum control. Your trigger finger should be straight and lie along the side of the frame or the outside of the trigger guard refer to Figure 4-4.

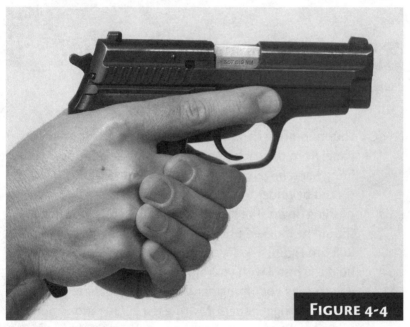

FIGURE 4-4

Safe ready position

B. Be sure to fit the "V" of your hand, formed by the thumb and the index finger of the shooting hand, as high as possible on the backstrap of the frame. This placement is to help manage recoil more efficiently. Your grip holding the pistol should align the backstrap of the pistol with the wrist and forearm.

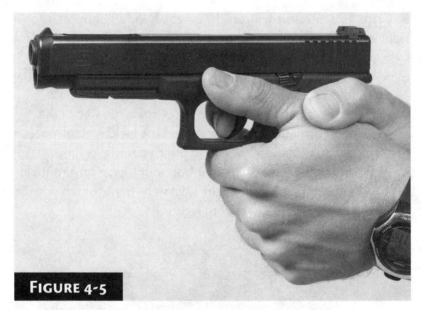

FIGURE 4-5

Placement of nonfiring hand

C. Your non-firing hand should now fill in the exposed grip
   panel from the back to the front to make a fist over your
   firing hand fingers. The thumb of your non-firing hand
   should be under the thumb of the firing hand, which is
   pushing down. The index finger of the non-firing hand
   should be indexed under the trigger guard, pushing up.
   Refer to Figure 4-5. Try to apply most of the tension to
   hold the pistol with your non-firing hand, which allows
   you to relax your firing hand and obtain greater control
   with your trigger finger. My rule is a 70/30 ratio of non-
   firing hand to firing hand tension. Others think that equal
   pressure (50/50) is more easily learned and works well
   for some. Use 100 percent of the grip panels; you can use
   skateboard tape to maximize friction. Pinch the heels of
   your hands together to get a complete grip. If you have
   extremely white knuckles or start trembling immediately,
   you are gripping too hard. You must find your happy
   medium, for this balance allows for sustained shooting if

the need arises. You will find the more you lock your wrists using the top tendon the more control you will have with recoil management.

D. The arms form a triangle, taking equal pressure in your position. The elbows are just under a full lock (keep it comfortable) to assist in allowing the recoil to go through the arms into your chest to help manage recoil. You may have to modify this grip and your elbows slightly as everyone has different hands and physical dimensions, and different pistols have various grips. Your grip must be consistently the same and comfortable. This isosceles of the arms is more natural to maintain under extremes than some forms of the Weaver technique. Train to use your natural instincts, not to counter them.

NOTE: Your grip will change as you become more proficient, and you should always check your grip before drifting any sights. Pistols come from the factory bench sighted in, and you should make your hand fit your pistol, not your pistol fit your hand. If you do this step correctly, you will be able to shoot quite well with any factory, out-of-the-box pistol. Try different pistols to learn which one fits you the best; there are many different grip angles out there, so check them out first.

4. **Breath control-** You must learn to hold your breath properly at any time during the breathing cycle if you wish to keep accuracy in stressful shooting situations. Remember that you must do this while aiming and squeezing the trigger. You must learn to inhale, then exhale normally, then hold your breath at the moment of the natural respiratory pause. Refer to Figure 4-6. The top diagram is of a single shot and the bottom diagram is a series of shots.

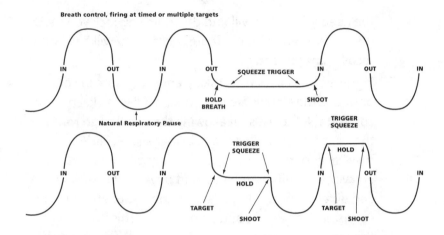

Breath control, firing at timed or multiple targets

FIGURE 4-6

This action allows you to steady your position with the front sight of the pistol at the precise aiming point while your breathing is paused. You must not hold your breath for more than 5-7 seconds. The lack of fresh oxygen causes blurred vision and trembling muscles. Beginners will have to take a breath in between a multiple-shot drill, but with practice, you will be able to shoot more with less breathing. Remember this is one of the fundamentals, and once you start to shoot faster and under more stress, you will have to manage your breathing and still get the job done.

5. **Sight alignment and sight picture:** I have combined these two considerations because they are very dependent on each other.

Sight alignment is centering the front sight into the rear sight notch. The top of the front sight must be level with the top of the rear sight and in alignment with the eye. When you see this point, you will notice that on either side of the front sight is visible light. Your alignment must be such that the light on the left is equal to the light on the right. The eye will normally do this, but be aware

FIGURE 4-7A & 4-7B

Sight Alignment

Sight Picture

of it when you start. Refer to Figure 4-7a.

Sight picture is taking this sight alignment and superimposing it onto your desired target. A correct sight picture is proper sight alignment with the front sight placed on the center of mass of the available target (your aiming point should be the size of the bullet you are firing). Remember that it is the center of mass of the available target, not a certain part of one's anatomy. If you see the whole person, it is his chest; if you see only his head, it is the center of that. Refer to Figure 4-7b. Since the eye can focus on only one object at different distances, you must focus on the front sight. Since the front sight is in clear focus (crystal clear with sharp edges and corners), your rear sight and target will be out of focus. Your front sight does not lie, so your bullet will go wherever your front sight was when you fired the shot. This point is handy in calling your shot, an educated guess as to where your bullet will go, since you saw the front sight lift off target when the pistol fired. You must keep both eyes open from the start of learning to shoot, thus allowing you to be more aware of your surroundings when you are aiming. You will need to begin using both eyes open because when you are stressed and in condition red, they will both be naturally open and not limiting your view. Train as you fight. Use your natural responses as you will have them with you.

SHOOTING FUNDAMENTALS

6. **Trigger control:** Accurate shooting depends greatly on your control of the trigger. Trigger press and sight alignment must be done at the same time while maintaining the minimum arc of movement to attain accurate shooting. This fundamental is the most commonly violated, so take note and learn it correctly.

A.   **Single-action:** First I will explain the single-action trigger control necessary to attain accuracy. The part of the index finger to be used is halfway from the tip to the first joint. This placement may change with time, as you will notice different bullet strikes when you place your finger differently on the trigger. Let's start with the beginner's trigger control. First you remove slack and apply initial pressure to the trigger once you are on your target. Settle into the aiming area and obtain the desired sight picture. Then begin applying a positive increase in pressure on the trigger, maintaining a smooth and even press to the rear without interruption. At first the shots should be a surprise to you. As you maintain your press to the rear, continue applying pressure on the trigger for a split second and release the trigger forward, only far enough to re-engage the sear, but do not allow your finger to lose contact with the trigger. Remove the slack and prepare for the next shot. It is paramount to concentrate on the front sight throughout the trigger press. Remember that where your front sight was when the shot was fired is exactly where your bullet will go. So it is good to focus on the front sight for accuracy and to know if you need to repeat the shot.

B.   **Double-action**- Double-action is more difficult to learn initially, but it may become very effective if used with correct practice. The problem most people have when firing double-action is that they are fully extended towards the target when they begin to take the slack out and begin their press towards the rear with the trigger. This practice accounts for most shots being pulled to the right since the trigger pull of most double-action pistols is quite heavy. To master fast and accurate double-action shooting, once you decide you are going to shoot, you must begin to take out the slack (muzzle towards the target from position three) and begin the steady press to the rear as the pistol is brought from position three to position four, both hands on the pistol with it pointed towards the target. As you extend toward the target, you are removing the slack and applying increased pressure on the trigger to have the shot break as soon as fully presented. This action allows for very fast and accurate shots since once the pistol is at full extension, very little pressure is needed to make the pistol fire. With practice, this action will be as fast as a single-action. This technique also allows you to begin shooting once you are at position three, and fire as you present the pistol to full extension. This technique is for advanced double-action shooting but is easily learned safely through proper dryfire. If in doubt, do not conduct double-action firing as described. Fully present to the target and have a

FIGURE 4-8A

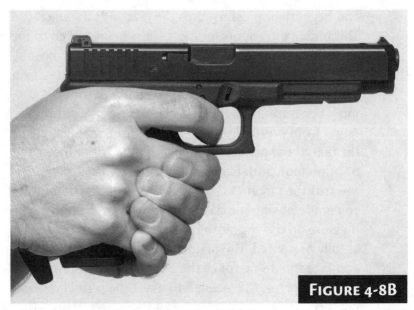

FIGURE 4-8B

Proper trigger finger placement

smooth and steady press to the rear of the trigger as you have proper a sight picture on the target.

C. **Glock Safe-Action System**- Think of this trigger action like a light double-action; learn how far you can press the trigger to the rear before it will fire. Practice the timing of the sights, extending your arms and the rearward trigger pressure. Notice the trigger finger does not touch the frame or trigger guard refer to Figure 4-8A & 4-8B.

NOTE: With either type of trigger, ensure that your trigger finger contacts the trigger only and not the frame, as it will move your bullet strike.

7. **Follow-through:** This step is the act of continuing to apply all the shooting fundamentals mentioned above throughout the break of the shot to prevent any unnecessary movement before the bullet leaves the barrel. The slightest movement will have

a dramatic effect on your bullet strike. You should maintain concentration on sight alignment even after the shot has been fired. If you do this step correctly, you will achieve a surprise shot with no reflexes of anticipation to disturb your sight alignment. Within follow-through is the act of recovery; the act of returning the pistol to the original holding position in the aiming area. If you use the proper stance, correct grip, and arm position, the recovery will be more natural and uniform. Proper recovery must be accomplished as quickly as possible by taking the recoil straight back from the pistol to the shoulders. As soon as the shot breaks, you must immediately resume the sequence of applying the fundamentals for the next shot (manage recoil, reacquire another sight picture, reset the sear (letting the trigger out just far enough to reset the sear, which allows the pistol to be able to fire again), and prep the trigger (learn how far the trigger can be pressed to the rear before it will fire) for a follow-up shot if needed). Think of follow-through three ways: mentally (your thought process of what happened and what is happening?), physically (discussed above as how to get the pistol back on target ready to re-engage), and tactically (what should I be doing to survive the engagement?).

8. **Conclusion of the shooting fundamentals:** These shooting fundamentals are just the basic instruction needed to continue with more advanced pistol learning. The coach-pupil method of teaching works well with these techniques if the teacher is knowledgeable in the application of the techniques. At this point, you may have to enlist an instructor because no book can see what you are doing incorrectly. Remember to dry fire five times for every one live fire practice; there is no need to waste your training resources on incorrect techniques. Ensure your pistol is clear before conducting dry fire practice.

PISTOL
PROFILE

SIG SAUER
MODEL: P226R

Caliber	Barrel Length	Overall Length	Nom. Weight	Magazine Capacity
9mm	4.98 "	8.60 "	1 lbs. 14 oz.	10 & 15

CHAPTER FIVE

SHOOTING POSITIONS

This chapter will explain the proper draw from a holster, various shooting positions and their uses. I will start with the steps to the full presentation from the holster, otherwise known as the draw sequence. It is broken into four steps. Each step is important for its own reasons, so it is essential to practice them exactly so they become reflex. The draw is essential to all other practical combat shooting.

THE FOUR-STEP PRESENTATION OF THE DRAW–

FIGURE 5-1A

FIGURE 5-1B

POSITION ONE: A threat is perceived and you decide you are going to draw and shoot, so you orient your stance towards the threat and begin your draw sequence. Quickly, your firing hand moves to begin forming its grip on the pistol grip; this is the only chance to get a proper grip. Index with the web of the firing hand high on the backstrap (set your firing hand as high as you can on the backstrap), extend the trigger finger straight, and then grip the pistol with the three lower fingers. Refer to Figure 5-1A and 5-1B. The thumb disengages the thumb break on the holster and then finishes to form the grip as you begin to pull the pistol from the holster. The non-firing hand is drawn to the body's centerline and is open to receive the pistol with fingers extended and joined oriented 45 degrees down. Only move what you must to accomplish these steps of the draw. Economy of effort and economy of motion allow you to do this quickly. Once you are comfortable with the correct step one, this step can be done as fast as possible as it is not a fine-motor function. This step is conducted at the fastest speed you can correctly do it.

FIGURE 5-2A

FIGURE 5-2B

POSITION TWO: Your firing hand has its proper grip on the pistol, and you draw the pistol from the holster. As soon as the pistol is clear from the holster, it is immediately pointed in the direction of the threat while moving to the centerline of the body to meet the non-firing hand. Refer to Figure 5-2A and 5-2B. The trigger finger can begin to take up slack in the trigger if you need to fire from the position of retention or an advancing threat at close ranges. As soon as you are pointing the muzzle at the threat, you can take the pistol off safe. As you move to position three, you may orient the pistol under your dominant eye to assist in picking up the front sight faster refer to Figure 5-3B. The speed of this step is also as fast as possible once properly learned.

FIGURE 5-3A

FIGURE 5-3B

POSITION THREE: Your non-firing hand begins to complete the two-handed grip, and the muzzle is directed toward your threat. In this position the finger is still off the trigger unless you intend to begin shooting. If the threat is closing or taking offensive actions and is within in your ability range, you may begin to engage from this position as you complete your presentation. This is our preferred **ready position**, with your finger off the trigger. The upper body must be semi-relaxed; watch tensing your trapezoids. Refer to Figure 5-3A. Also, do not hunch your head forward; keep it naturally erect to a slight bit forward (keep it comfortable).

NOTE: From position three to four, the slack and tension are taken out of the double-action pistols. And at full presentation is when the shot should break and fire to attain great accuracy and speed.

NOTE: The pressing of the hands and pistol forward from position three to position four is at a medium speed (allowing you time to press your trigger and acquire the sight picture desired). Smoothness must be emphasized to time the shot correctly at

FIGURE 5-4A

FIGURE 5-4B

full extension—the trigger press, movement, sight alignment, and sight picture all come together at full extension with a properly placed shot.

POSITION FOUR: This position is considered full presentation, and your most accurate shooting will be done from this position. Refer to Figure 5-4A and 5-4B. If you have time, review your shooting fundamentals before the shot. Do not maintain this position for long unless the situation requires it. Optimum time is no more than 6-8 seconds after your engagement. Once the engagement is complete, remove your finger from the trigger (only if the problem has been dealt with; remember to reset the trigger in your follow-through if the engagement is not complete) and take a breath in and exhale. Then scan and assess the situation; you should lower your muzzle 1 to 2 inches and look with three eyes (your two and your muzzle) by turning your head left and then right and then back to center. Actually see and analyze what is happening—you must turn your head (to the left, to the right, or wherever you need to look) as you look so you break the tunnel vision that is common in high-stress situations. When you bring the weapon back to position three, you should check the condition of your weapon (ensure it is in battery), decock and/engage the safety on your pistol, and then look over your shoulders to check behind you; this puts you in a good position if you must turn and engage or fight. To rest, you should go to the low-ready position or back to position three of the draw.

FIGURE 5-5

Low ready

LOW-READY POSITION: This position is used to assess a situation after you have fully presented, deemed the situation is slowing, or need to rest and assess refer to Figure 5-5. Many use this for range practice as a position for resting between drills; this should not be done as a standard operating procedure. Use position three of the draw sequence refer to Figures 5-3A and 5-3B. I advocate using position three of the draw for resting and waiting, as you are immediately ready to begin to fire if necessary. In a shooting situation, it is used to remain ready and allow you to see what is in front of you, yet be ready to engage very quickly. MUZZLE TOWARD THREAT OR THREAT AREA!

Left and Below:
One-knee
Variations

FIGURE 5-6A

FIGURE 5-6B

KNEELING POSITION: This position is very tactically sound since it may be used to hide behind available cover, and you can come out from the left, right, or over to engage threats. The position shown in Figure 5-6A allows the shooter to stand back up and move if necessary. The position shown in Figure 5-6B is good for distant threats when you are behind good cover and you can go to the prone position easily. You can also go down on either knee and maintain 90-degree angles with your legs for stability as in Figure 5-6A. When you go to this position from the standing position all you need to do is replace your foot with your knee to go quickly and consistently to a kneeling position.

You also may take a kneeling position, depending on which side your spare magazines are stored on your kit for easy reach. For shooting around cover you put the knee down on the side you are shooting around (shooting around to the right you put your right knee down, this limits your exposure). Your body type has a lot to do with how you take a kneeling position or whether you take a kneeling position at all. Refer to Figure 5-7A to see a two-knee-down variation. You may also practice with the use of your primary weapon (shotgun or rifle) and figure out how you want to take a kneeling position to allow you to get to your pistol if a transition is needed. The kneeling position may also be taken to shoot a high-angle shot in a close and crowded situation to clear your area behind the target and bullet path refer to Figure 5-7B.

Two knees down kneeling and high-angle shot

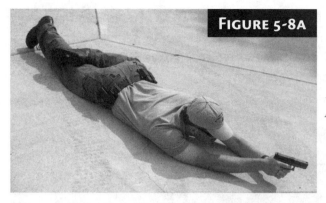

FIGURE 5-8A

Rollover prone position

FIGURE 5-8B

Traditional prone position

PRONE POSITION: This position is a very steady, low-profile position from which to fire. The key is to practice this technique as detailed and not to become lazy. The rollover prone position places the firing arm in line with the body to provide maximum recoil management and low profile. If you need some height to get the correct sight picture, you can use one of your knees to raise the weapon. Do it the old cowboy way (as in Figure 5-8B) and rest on your elbows, and you lose your recoil management advantages of the position in Figure 5-8A. Remember to practice getting to your magazines and correcting malfunctions in the prone positions. Both positions are quite useful for different situations; practice them to find which one works for you. To go into a prone position from the standing or kneeling positions, place your non-firing hand on the ground slightly ahead of where you want your torso to lay and manage your descent to the ground.

DRAWING FROM A SEATED POSTION: The draw is the same as if standing. Notice that the draw sequence is identical to the standing draw. Refer to Figures 5-9A through 5-9D. Consistency equals accuracy.

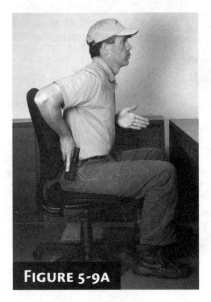

FIGURE 5-9A

FIGURE 5-9B

FIGURE 5-9C

FIGURE 5-9D

FIGURE 5-10

SITTING POSITION: The sitting position can be used when the situation allows. You are limited in your mobility, but with the appropriate cover, it is a very steady position. Notice in Figure 5-10 that the bones of the elbow are resting against the inside of the knee joint, skeletal support as opposed to using your muscles to hold the position. Using skeletal support allows you to maintain this position longer without suffering muscular fatigue. Remember, shooting over cover is not always the best utilization of the cover, but the situation also dictates your choices.

FIGURE 5-11A

Full flat-foot supine position

FIGURE 5-11B

SUPINE POSITION: Supine shooting may be used when fighting from the ground, whether wounded or just off your base. Be careful not to shoot your own feet; lay them as flat to the ground, refer to Figures 5-11A and 5-11B) as you can and be aware of their location if tracking a target. You may also use the bent- knee version of the supine position (Figure 5-11C); be aware of the location of your knees. Nothing hurts worse than a self-induced wound, mentally and physically. From this position you can rotate on your back to reorient to a new or moving threat as needed. It also allows your legs to assist in protecting your torso from direct impacts.

Bent-knee variation of the supine position

FIGURE 5-11C

FIGURE 5-12A   FIGURE 5-12B

Strong-hand shooting for a right hand-dominant shooter

STRONG-HAND SHOOTING POSITION: This position is used to fire your pistol with only the strong shooting hand. It may be used when you are shooting while wounded or while holding something that is obviously more important than your steady two-hand shooting grip. With this position, you must turn your strong side toward the threat so that your arm is aligned with your chest. Notice the stance opens up with a slight step forward. Refer to Figures 5-12A and 5-12B. This puts the side of your chest behind your shooting arm. This position allows the recoil to be sent into your upper torso as you slightly bend towards your threat from the waist. It is very important to tighten the wrist to unify your firing arm. Your pistol is slightly canted (45 degrees at most) to the left or as normally held—as straight up as normal. The 45-degree cant allows you to steady the pistol with the stronger muscles of your forearm and locks out your wrist to prevent it from bucking with recoil. You need to practice this position in order for you to determine your sight picture. Some may have to aim slightly low and to the right to hit their center of mass. While practicing or firing with a wounded non-firing arm, you should draw it up to your chest to allow you to steady your body's movement.

FIGURE 5-13A   **FIGURE 5-13B**

Weak (non-firing) hand shooting for a right hand-dominant shooter

WEAK-HAND SHOOTING POSITION: This position is used to fire your pistol with only the weak, non-shooting hand. It may be used when you are shooting or practicing to shoot while wounded. With this position, you must turn your non-firing side toward the threat so that your arm is aligned with your chest. Notice the stance opens up refer to Figures 5-13A and 5-13B toward the threat, which puts the side of your chest behind your shooting arm. This placement allows the recoil to be sent into your upper torso, which is slightly bent towards your threat. Again, it is very important to tighten the wrist to unify your firing arm. Your pistol is slightly canted (45 degrees at most) to the right or as normally held—as straight up as normal. The 45-degree cant allows you to steady the pistol with the stronger muscles of your forearm and locks out your wrist to prevent it from bucking with recoil. You should practice this position in order for you to determine your sight picture. Some may have to aim slightly low and to the left to hit their center of mass. While practicing or firing with a wounded strong arm, you should draw it up to your chest to allow you to steady your body's movement.

NOTE: You will be moving in a modified position three, and when you need to shoot, you will press to position four as if standing still. Exception to this is shooting at very close ranges using weapon retention techniques. Trigger finger is off the trigger until you have intent to shoot.

FIGURE 5-14A

FIGURE 5-14B

FIGURE 5-14C

FIGURE 5-14D

Moving Forward

MOVING FORWARD: At times you should close in on a threat and not waste time in stopping to take the shot. The key to moving and shooting is to move only as fast as you can effectively engage. This is explained as a "careful hurry." When moving forward, use a heel plant and roll the foot to the toes and take the next step. Lower the body with some bend in the knees to act as shock absorbers. Refer to Figure 5-14A–5-14D. You may also have to shorten your steps. You are trying to move from the waist down and not have your head bobbing as your weapon will also be bobbing. This is a learned skill to build confidence to move quickly and still attain your desired accuracy. Continue to practice magazine changes and malfunction drills while moving. Practicing when you actually break the shot (feet on ground or one in the air) must be decided upon by the shooter. You should not have to stop to fire effectively under 25 meters on a full silhouette-sized target.

FIGURE 5-15   FIGURE 5-15

Moving Backwards

MOVING BACKWARDS: No one likes to talk about moving backwards in a tactical situation, but sometimes it is necessary. We will not discuss why you are moving backwards, but the most sensible way to do so. To maintain sight of an area or threat, you decide you do not want to lose security by turning and running. Identify where you are going and determine the best pace at which to get there. Study the ground for any obstacles and re-orient toward the threat area or threat and begin to move backwards by sliding your rearward foot along the ground, feeling for any obstacles that may cause you to trip and fall refer to Figure 5-15. Alternate feet until you get to where you want to go and continue with your plan; your forward foot should not slide past your planted foot. Hazards of moving backwards are obvious and should be conducted as safely as possible as the situaion dictates.

FIGURE 5-16

Shooting to the sides

SHOOTING LATERAL TO MOVEMENT: This can easily be done by just turning your upper body (your tank turret) toward the threat and engaging refer to Figure 5-16. You may decide you need to slow down at the break of the shot, but you should practice so you know how fast you may go to continue movement. If you begin to turn too much away from your direction of movement, you may have to turn toward the threat as the situation dictates. And depending on the situation, you may choose to shoot to the sides with a one-hand technique. The circumstances may require it. Survival modifies many learned skills.

SIDESTEPPING: Sidestepping is used when you "pie off" (to look tactically around visual barriers incrementally, exposing minimal body parts) an area. You do not want to step across your feet as there is more of a chance of tripping over one's own feet. Move the foot on the side you want to go in that direction and then bring your trailing foot over and continue. Refer to Figures 5-17A through 5-17D. This shooter is moving to his left). It is related to the slide and drag used to move to the rear. Do not lift your feet if you do not have too; slide them to avoid losing balance from contacting an obstacle.

Sidestepping shooter stepping to his right.

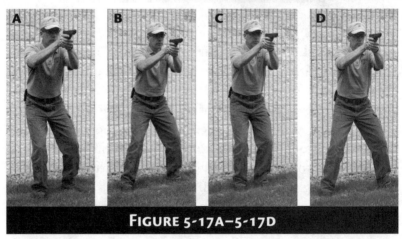

FIGURE 5-17A–5-17D

FIGURE 5-18

Bending the wrist in position three to avoid flagging with the muzzle.

MUZZLE DIRECTION DURING MOVEMENTS: If you are moving with your weapon in the low-ready or position three, you must be aware as to what your muzzle is pointing. You can safely move this way if you pay attention to those around you that do not need a muzzle pointed at them. If a non-threatening individual is crossing your muzzle, bend your wrists down to orient the muzzle to the ground until he is out of the way, then bring the muzzle back up. Refer to Figure 5-18. Be very cognizant as to your muzzle direction. At no time should it be oriented at anything you are not willing to destroy. Practice this even with training weapons or dry rehearsals so it will be second nature. Those around you will appreciate it.

FIGURE 5-19A

FIGURE 5-19B

FIGURE 5-19C

*Photos of a
90-degree
pivot turn*

FIGURE 5-19D

FIGURE 5-19E

TURNING 90 DEGREES: You can turn 90 degrees while standing or moving in basically the same way. Pivot on the ball of the foot for the direction you want to turn and place the other foot in your normal stance once your turn is almost complete. Refer to Figures 5-19A through 5-19E. You Perceive a threat (so you turn your head to look), Recognize it is a threat (begin your turn), and Acquire the threat (with your sights) in preparation to shoot. This is a P.R.A. drill used to perceive, recognize, and acquire a threat to the one side or the other.

FIGURE 5-20A   FIGURE 5-20B   FIGURE 5-20C

FIGURE 5-20D   FIGURE 5-20E   FIGURE 5-20F

TURNING 180 DEGREES: Turning around 180-degrees is normally conducted from a static standing position and is similar to the 90-degree turn previously discussed refer to Figures 5-20A through 5-20F. Why turn to begin with? You <u>Perceive</u> a threat (so you turn your head to look), <u>Recognize</u> it is a threat (begin your turn), and <u>Acquire</u> the threat (with your sights) in preparation to shoot. This is a P.R.A. drill used to perceive, recognize, and acquire a threat to the rear. Remember the direction you turn your head to look is the direction you will be turning your body. Refer to Figure 5-20A. And as with a 90-degree turn, you will be pivoting on the ball of the foot that you are turning (turning left- pivot on the ball of the left foot and vice versa for turning right). Refer to Figure 5-20B. Your outboard foot should come to a stop in the normal shooting stance so you are ready to engage as if you were already facing that direction. Refer to Figure 5-20C. If drawing during the turn, do not bring your muzzle horizontal to the ground until you are oriented toward the threat.

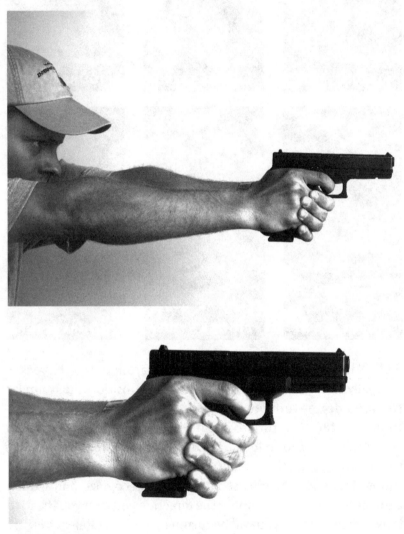

A solid grip keeps you on target during recoil.

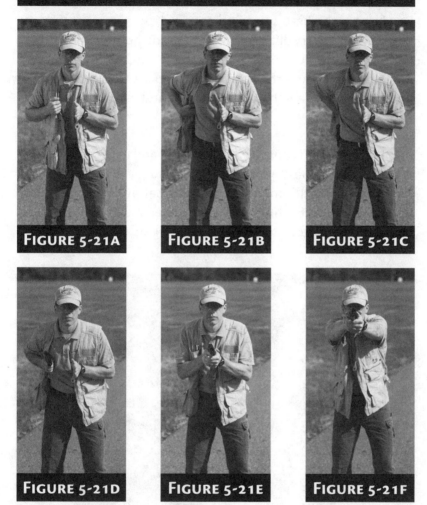

FIGURE 5-21A   **FIGURE 5-21B**   **FIGURE 5-21C**

FIGURE 5-21D   **FIGURE 5-21E**   **FIGURE 5-21F**

Series of a concealed draw from under a jacket.

NOTE: When beginning to sweep the jacket, it is better to start up high at the collar area and sweep in and down to avoid getting a handful of jacket instead of the grip refer to Figures 5-21A and 5-21B. Doing this also does not tip your hand if you are surprised and begin to draw and then decide not to.

The only difference in drawing from concealment is getting to your pistol; other than that aspect, it is a normal four-step draw. Dry firing is the best way to practice a draw from concealment. You may have to try different carry methods, holsters, or pistols to find one with which you are comfortable and confident enough. Remember, you carry them more than you use them, so you must find a happy medium between comfort and practicality.

NOTE: To remain concealed, the holster and magazine pouches must remain behind your hip bone (kidney area) to prevent flashing your equipment during normal activities. Refer to figure 5-22A-5-22B. This also aids in immediate muzzle-to-target orientation as you are not twisting the sights up.

FIGURE 5-22A

FIGURE 5-22B

Photos of equipment placement for concealment.

FIGURE 5-23A

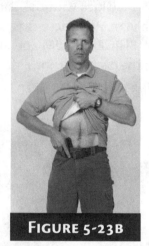

FIGURE 5-23B

FIGURE 5-23C

FIGURE 5-23D

FIGURE 5-23E

Series of a "Rip and Grip" concealed draw.

"Rip and Grip" Felony Carry Method (shirt not tucked in)

NOTE: When the shirt is ripped up to allow the firing hand to get a grip, the non-firing hand is in the location needed to complete the two-handed grip at step three of a normal draw sequence. Ensure you slide your firing hand thumb well behind the pistol as you begin to form your grip refer to Figure 5-23B.

Obviously you do not want your finger near the trigger as noted before or during the actual draw part of the presentation. This is a very good carry for a Glock with the Carry Clip from Skyline Toolworks, LLC in Malvern, PA. These carry clips may be ordered off the web at WWW.BHIGEAR.COM and are installed onto the slide without tools so the pistol will not slide from your waistband during normal activities.

Above: Carry Clip from Skyline Tools, LLC
Below: Glock with Saf-T-Blok

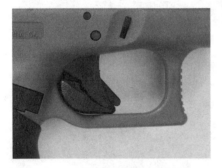

I also suggest using a Saf-T-Blok from Concept Development Corporation for use on carrying the Glock pistol in this manner. The Saf-T-Blok reduces the possibility of accidental discharges when carrying unconventionally, like in a fanny pack, tucked in a belt, or in your pocket. It snaps into place behind the trigger, providing a positive trigger block. And when the pistol is needed, it ejects instantly by pushing the Saf-T-Blok ejector with the index finger. The Saf-T-Blok is also available at the above mentioned Webstore.

FIGURE 5-26A

FIGURE 5-26B

FIGURE 5-26C

FIGURE 5-26D

Series of a "Sparrow Team"(shirt tucked in)-type concealed draw

NOTE: This carry method has been employed as far back as the OSS and most recently by a Philippine terrorist group for assassination teams. This method has the individual carrying the pistol in front of his/her pants without a holster. The key point is to push up on the muzzle with the nonfiring fingers to allow for aquiring a proper grip as you draw refer to Figure 5-26B. KEEP YOUR FINGER OFF THE TRIGGER TILL ON TARGET AND READY TO SHOOT.

PISTOL
PROFILE

WALTHER
MODEL: P99

Caliber	Barrel Length	Overall Length	Nom. Weight	Magazine Capacity
9mm	4"	7 "	1 lbs. 9 oz.	10+1 / 16+1
.40 S&W	4.12"	7.12 "	1 lbs. 9 oz.	10+1 / 12+1

CHAPTER SIX

RELOADING TECHNIQUES

The act of reloading is an overlooked issue in most training, but it is true that shooters are killed due to dropping magazines, shaking hands, placing the magazine in backwards, and placing empty magazines back into the pistol. The stress induced by a life-threatening situation causes shooters to do things that they would not otherwise do. Consistent and repeated training that is properly performed is needed to avoid such mistakes.

1. Develop a consistent method for carrying magazines in the ammunition pouches. All magazines should face down with the bullets facing forward and to the center of the body. Your pouches should properly secure your magazines during strenuous actions.

2. Never practice an administrative reload. On the initial load, perform a speed reload. Be slow and technically correct to begin with and speed will come, but it is critical to practice with proper technique so as not to practice bad habits into routine.

3. Know when to reload. When possible, perform the tactical reload since it is safer to reload with a round in the chamber, which can be fired in an emergency. And you do not have to release the slide as when reloading from a slide lock. In a fight, reload when you can, not when you are forced to. Think tactically and ask yourself if you have the time and the opportunity to do it; if so, then perform a tactical reload.

4. Obtain the proper grip on the magazine to be loaded. This grip precludes the magazine being dropped or difficulty in placing the magazine into the pistol. Use the index finger to guide the magazine into the pistol. You must force yourself to shift focus momentarily to ensure you put the magazine into the magazine well correctly every time.

Practice these techniques under some type of stress. It may be through competitions, noise, after physical exercises — whatever gets your heart to pound — and you will then have to learn to calm yourself.

Reloading the semi-automatic magazine-fed pistol is broken down into the tactical reload and the speed reload. In this section, both will be explained.

TACTICAL RELOAD: The tactical reload is used to reload your pistol– either with a fully loaded or almost fully loaded magazine – before you move or anticipate a renewed assault on your position. This movement is a controlled one, so you will maintain control of both the magazine being replaced and the one replacing it. It should be performed from behind cover if tactically feasible and before you run out of ammo and experience a slide lock to the rear. Remember to think tactically and ask yourself if you have the time and the opportunity to do it; if so then perform a tactical reload.

FIGURE 6-1A

FIGURE 6-1B

Step one of tactical reload

<u>STEP ONE:</u> Once you have decided you are going to perform a tactical reload, you maintain security toward your threat area with the pistol and your eyes. Ensure your finger is off the trigger, and with your non-firing hand, properly draw a fresh magazine from your pouch. Refer to Figures 6-1A and 6-1B. To draw a magazine properly, extend your index finger along the front (the side of the magazine that the bullets are pointing at) of the magazine and pinch the sides with your thumb and middle finger.

FIGURE 6-2A   **FIGURE 6-2B**

Step two of tactical reload

STEP TWO: While maintaining the proper grip on the fresh magazine, slightly rotate the pistol in your hand so you may push the magazine release to drop the used magazine. With your non-firing hand, you will pinch the used magazine with the ring and pinkie fingers, then withdraw the used magazine from the pistol. Refer to Figure 6-2A. You may have to shift your vision quickly to the pistol to ensure that the exchange is completed smoothly, but then you must reshift your attention back to the threat area. While holding both magazines in the non-firing hand, insert the fresh magazine into the magazine well of the pistol. Maintain eye, muzzle, and threat alignment to speed and ease the re-engagement. Refer to Figure 6-2B. This may not be comfortable for individuals with small hands and large-capacity magazines. Remember that under great stress, this technique may be difficult to do, so you must practice until it is reflex-like.

FIGURE 6-3A   **FIGURE 6-3B**

Step three of tactical reload

STEP THREE: Once the magazine is halfway into the magazine well, firmly seat it with the palm of the non-firing hand. Notice where the pistol is in relation to your body; it maintains the eye, muzzle, and target line to minimize movement and speed up your re-acquiring of the sight onto target if needed. Refer to Figure 6-3A. Once the pistol is loaded, you may stow the used magazine somewhere other than where you have the fully loaded ones—front pocket, back pocket, or a belt pouch, but do not keep it in your teeth or in your hand. Refer to Figure 6-3B.

SPEED RELOAD: The speed reload is used when you have shot all the rounds in your pistol and your slide is locked to the rear. Unlike the tactical reload, which is moderately slow, the speed reload relies on speed to reload your pistol so you can continue the fight. Learning it will be done slowly so you perform the steps correctly; speed will come with practice. Keep a straight line with your eye, muzzle, and target when you are bringing the pistol back toward your face so you can quickly and easily roll the pistol back on to target and pick up the front sight quickly.

FIGURE 6-4A

Step one of speed reload

FIGURE 6-4B

STEP ONE: When you realize that your slide is locked to the rear because it is empty, you must immediately shift the pistol in your strong hand so you may reach and activate the magazine release with your firing-hand thumb refer to Figure 6-4A. At the same time, your non-firing hand will quickly go to the centerline of your body and move left along the belt to your magazine pouch. Refer to Figure 6-4B. With the non-firing hand index finger extended on the front of the magazine, pinch the first magazine you touch with your thumb and middle fingers. Refer to Figure 6-5. This pinch allows you to control the removal of the magazine from the pouch and position it for insertion into the pistol.

NOTE: Your magazine pouch will determine how you execute this step. If it is snapped or fastened with Velcro, incorporate this detail into the step to smooth out your magazine removal.

NOTE: If the magazine in the pistol does not drop, you will have to strip it from the magazine well. To do this step, you use the edge of the fresh magazine to put pressure on the baseplate of the stuck magazine. An alternative method is to pinch the stuck magazine with the pinkie and ring fingers, pull it out and drop it, then continue to reload the pistol.

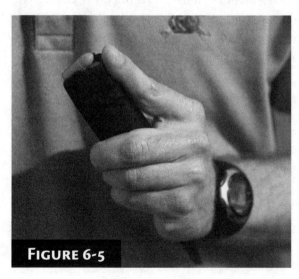

Showing the non-firing hand grip on a magazine for reload reload

FIGURE 6-5

Step two of speed reload

STEP TWO: Once the magazine has fallen from the pistol to the ground and the fresh magazine is on its way to the magazine well, with the magazine well rotated back toward your face, you need to prepare to "thread the needle." Refer to Figure 6-6B. Ensure you can slightly see the open hole of the magazine well on your quick peek to ensure the magazine is going to hit the hole. Maintain your eye, muzzle, and target alignment.

FIGURE 6-7A

FIGURE 6-7B

Step three of speed reload

FIGURE 6-7C

Continuation of: Step three of speed reload

STEP THREE: As you begin to insert the fresh magazine, glance at the magazine well to ensure the extended index finger guides the magazine into the well. As soon as half of the magazine is in the magazine well, immediately refocus on the threat. Vigorously seat the magazine in the pistol with the heel of the non-firing hand, ensuring you have a hard palm with your fingers extended. Refer to Figure 6-7B. Disengage the slide release with your firing

FIGURE 6-8

Continuation of: Step three of speed reload

hand thumb and allow the slide to close by its own spring tension. Refer to Figure 6-7C.

An alternative may be for you to "slingshot" the slide by gripping the rear serrations of the slide with your non-firing hand thumb and index finger and pulling the slide to the rear, then letting it return by its own spring tension. Refer to Figure 6-8. If you use the "slingshot" technique, pivot the pistol on the bore (right-handed shooters pivot the slide to the left) to have the slide meet your non-firing hand. Grasp the rear serrations of the slide, pull the slide slightly rear, and release. Regrip into your two-handed grip as you roll your sights back up and present back to the threat.

STEP FOUR: Reform your grip and continue the engagement. Refer to Figures 6-9A and 6-9B. If you keep your eye, muzzle, and target alignment, it is simple to re-acquire your front sight quickly as you regrip. A good time for a speed reload (position three to four, one shot, reload, and shoot) is 3 to 3.5 seconds on a full silhouette-sized target at 7 meters, depending on the type of magazine pouch you are using.

FIGURE 6-9A

FIGURE 6-9B

Step four of speed reload

RELOAD FROM CONCEALMENT

FIGURE 6-7C

Drawing a magazine from concealment

NOTE: Refer to chapter five on the draw from concealment for sweeping motion to get back to your magazines every time so you can feed that hogleg. Figure 6-10 shows reloading from concealment.

PISTOL
PROFILE

SMITH & WESSON

MODEL: SW99

Caliber	Barrel Length	Overall Length	Nom. Weight	Magazine Capacity
9mm	3.5 " & 4 "	6.6" & 7.125"	23–25.4 oz.	8+1 / 10+1
.40 S&W	3.5 " & 4.125 "	6.6" & 7.25 "	22.5–25.2 oz.	10+1
.45 ACP	4.25 "	7.5 "	25.6 oz.	9+1

CHAPTER SEVEN

MALFUNCTION DRILLS

Malfunctions are usually preventable through good practice, but they may still occur out of the blue from time to time. Of course, you hope it is on the practice range, but you should treat each one as if you are in a life-or-death situation. Practicing proper and effective corrective actions will allow you to be more confident in your pistol handling. In stressful situations, you can become much more stressed due to an unforeseen malfunction that is easily remedied. I have observed many shooters that perceive themselves to be experienced, but when they encounter a stovepipe, they nearly disassemble the pistol rather than sweep it out and continue.

Proper training will do more to save your life than technology and the arms race to be bigger and better. Malfunction drills must fix the problem 100 percent of the time (excluding a weapon stoppage—broken weapon) the first time performed. You must look at the pistol and identify the problem. Obviously the pistol is not functioning as you need, so you must transition to another weapon or rectify the situation. It is a non-functioning weapon at this point—fix it.

Whether you take a kneeling position to correct malfunctions is up to you, depending on the situation or how you operate. If you do and others are around you with weapons, let them know you are going to stand back up by whatever means you have prearranged.

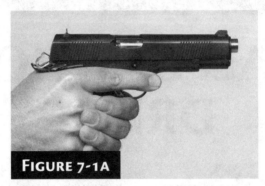

FIGURE 7-1A

Failure to go into battery

NOTE: The failure-to-go-into-battery malfunction, when your slide does not fully return forward when cycling a round, is always rectified in the same manner, no matter which hand is being used. This malfunction is usually induced when loading and not allowing the full recoil spring tension to shut the slide. Refer to Figure 7-1A.

FIGURE 7-1B

Seating the side

To fix a failure-to-go-into-battery malfunction, you must ensure your finger is off the trigger and outside the trigger guard and then slap the back of the slide with the heel of the non-firing hand.

Refer to Figure 7-1B. If you are shooting while wounded, then you will use your chest or equipment to force the slide forward into battery.

FAILURE TO FIRE-TYPE I- This malfunction occurs when the operator has loaded a dud cartridge or failed to load the chamber. The universal fix all for this is the "Slap, Rack, Ready" technique.

Failure to fire–Type I

SYMPTOM- You perform a full presentation to shoot and hear and feel the hammer strike, but the weapon does not fire. Refer to Figure 7-2. Before performing this correction you must remove your trigger finger from the trigger.

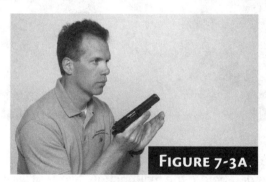

Slap

1. **SLAP** the bottom of the magazine with a hard palm (fingers extended) to ensure it is fully seated and locked in. Refer to Figure 7-3A.

FIGURE 7-3B

Rack

2. **RACK** the slide fully to the rear and release it to shut by its own recoil spring tension. You can pivot the slide toward your non-firing hand on the axis of the bore. This can speed up and assist in racking the slide to the rear. Maintain muzzle-to-threat orientation. Refer to Figure 7-3B.

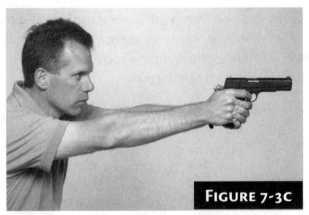

FIGURE 7-3C

Ready

3. **READY** or re-present and prepare to fire the shot as you intended before the malfunction if your situation dictates that action. Refer to Figure 7-3C.

FAILURE TO EJECT-TYPE II: This malfunction (commonly called a "stovepipe") is created usually by the slide being retarded by not setting one's wrists ("limp wristing") in its rearward movement to rechamber the next round or by a broken ejector. Refer to Figure 7-4. This malfunction is easily corrected by sweeping the expended case from the port. The corrective action is the same for vertical and horizontal stovepipes.

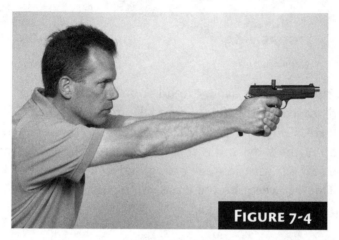

FIGURE 7-4

Stovepipe–Type II

SYMPTOM: You are in the act of shooting a multiple-round engagement, and you notice you cannot see your front sight for a piece of brass in the way, know the slide did not fully close, and/or have a soft, mushy trigger.

FIGURE 7-5A

Vertical Stovepipe example

FIGURE 7-5B

Horizontal Stovepipe example

FIGURE 7-6A

Reach across

FIGURE 7-6B

Rearward sweep

With the non-firing hand, extend your fingers, and with fingers joined, reach over the slide. Refer to Figure 7-6A. DO NOT SWEEP YOUR HAND IN FRONT OF THE MUZZLE. Roll your fingers over the top of the slide, and with a firm, vigorous sweeping motion to the rear against the stuck casing, sweep it free refer to Figure 7-6B. Do not sweep this too far as you have to take more time to regrip and present.

FIGURE 7-6C

Completion of the sweep

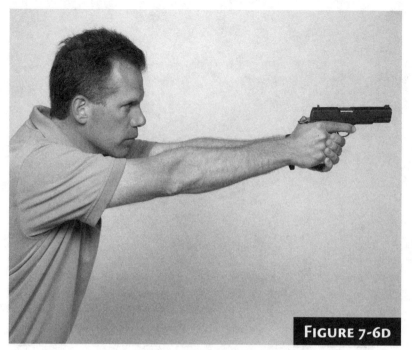

FIGURE 7-6D

Present and fire

Once the casing is no longer pinched by the slide, the slide will continue to seat the next round, and you are now ready to continue the engagement. Refer to Figure 7-6C. Many inexperienced shooters do too much to correct this simple malfunction. **Ensure you do not work the slide fully to the rear when sweeping the empty casing—this could induce a double feed as the chamber is already loaded.** Continue the engagement as your situation dictates. Refer to Figure 7-6B.

NOTE: You must always roll your fingers across so that whichever malfunction you encounter, vertical or horizontal, you will clear it with one sweep.

FIGURE 7-7

Failure to Extract–Type III

FAILURE-TO-EXTRACT-TYPE III: This malfunction
(commonly called a "double feed") is created when the spent
casing is not extracted from the chamber, and the next round to
be loaded is rammed from the magazine into the rear of the stuck
casing. Refer to Figures 7-7 and 7-8. This malfunction is a serious
one since dexterity and movement are needed to correct it and, of
course, to do it quickly. Below is the breakdown of the corrective
action to restore your pistol back to operation.

SYMPTOM: You are shooting a multiple shot engagement and
notice your slide did not go forward, you have a soft, mushy trigger,
and it will not fire.

STEP ONE: With your finger off the trigger, rotate the pistol in your
firing hand so you may engage the slide release with your firing-hand
thumb. With the non-firing hand, rack the slide to the rear and lock
it with the slide release by pushing it up into the notch, and let the

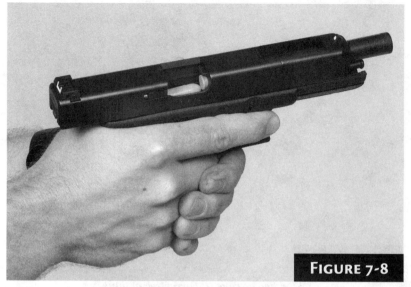

Failure to Extract malfunction

recoil spring tension hold the slide release in the notch. Refer to Figure 7-9A. The slide is locked to the rear first so as to release the recoil spring's tension on the malfunction; this works every time to assist in correcting this malfunction.

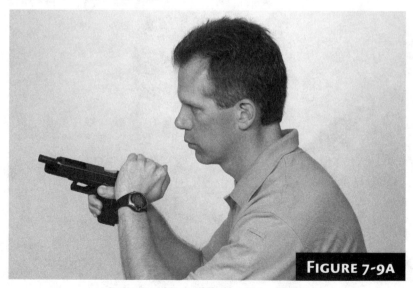

Step one of Type III corrective actions

MALFUNCTION DRILLS

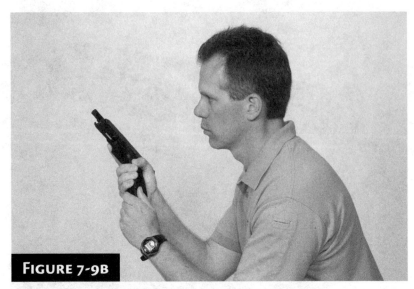

FIGURE 7-9B

Step two of Type III corrective actions

STEP TWO: Remove the magazine from the pistol. Refer to Figure 7-9B.

STEP THREE: Rack the slide to the rear at least two times to ensure the casing is extracted and ejected from the pistol. As you are

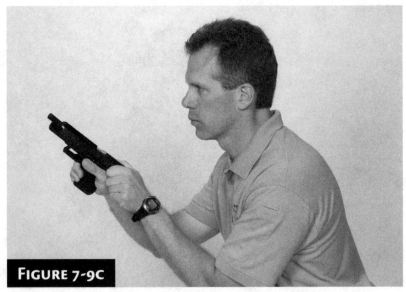

FIGURE 7-9C

Step two of Type III corrective actions

doing this, observe the casing being ejected and allow the slide to use its force to shut each time it is pulled to the rear. Refer to Figure 7-9C. You can rotate the slide towards your non-firing hand to assist in working the slide to the rear.

STEP FOUR- Properly insert and seat a loaded magazine with a hard palm. Refer to Figures 7-9D and 7-9E.

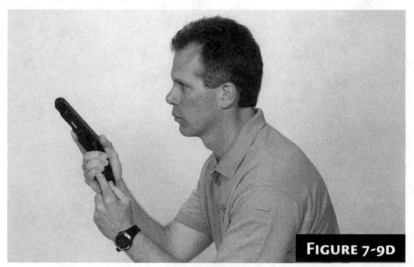

FIGURE 7-9D

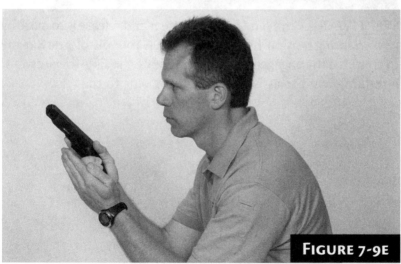

FIGURE 7-9E

Step four of Type III corrective actions

FIGURE 7-9F

Step five of Type III corrective actions

STEP FIVE- Rack the slide fully to the rear and release it to close by its own spring tension. Refer to Figure 7-9F. Your pistol is now ready to continue the engagement. You can rotate the slide towards your non-firing hand to assist in working the slide to the rear.

FIGURE 7-9G

Step six of Type III corrective actions

STEP SIX- Continue the engagement as the situation dictates. Refer to Figure 7-9G.

NOTE: Correcting this malfunction needs to be practiced often since it is the most complicated to do under stress when you lose dexterity because blood is leaving the extremities to supply the major organs with fresh oxygen. Be sure to lock the slide to the rear **FIRST** so you will consistently correct this malfunction 100 percent of the time.

RUGER
MODEL: P95DAO

Caliber	Barrel Length	Overall Length	Nom. Weight	Magazine Capacity
9mm Luger	3.9 "	7.25 "	1 lbs. 11 oz.	10+1

CHAPTER EIGHT

COMBAT MARKSMANSHIP

CONSIDERATIONS– TRAINING TIPS AND DRILLS

After you become proficient in the fundamentals of marksmanship, you will progress to combat marksmanship. The main objective of combat marksmanship is the use of the pistol to engage threats at close range with quick and accurate fire. In a gunfight, it is not the first round fired that wins, but the **first accurately fired round**. You should always use the sights when engaging the threat, the only exception being if this step would place the pistol within arm's reach of the threat.

Tactical Survival Rules:

1. Use your senses—our eyes and ears can be of great advantage if used to detect sights and smells that are not normal. Slow down or stop periodically to listen for any noise that is not normal in that environment.

2. Never turn your back on any uncleared area—you must systematically clear during your search of an area. This rule applies indoors and outdoors.

3. Keep your balance—never move faster than you can accurately shoot. Leaping around corners and sliding down hallways is not tactically feasible.

4. Stay away from corners—use angles to maintain an advantage. Pie off corners and be ready to fight when the situation allows it; maintain some distance to increase your reaction time.

5. Use and maximize the distance—use distance to your advantage and do not hug a danger area or assailant. The closer you are to a threat, the easier it is for them to hit you or attack you. Trust your ability when it comes to the range to the threat.

6. Take the initiative and/or advantage—at every point in a gunfight you should be taking advantage of whatever you can to fight and survive. Good losers are dead.

7. Do not remain static—move when the situation allows it, i.e., move after shooting, during magazine changes, and/or malfunction corrections. But be careful not to move and draw attention to yourself if the situation does not allow it.

8. Your wardrobe—watch what you wear, i.e., a light-colored shirt is nice to present a front sight onto. Try for the darker colors, depending on the area of operations.

9. Maintain your alertness—you should not be surprised. If you are searching for an individual, do not be shocked when you finally find him/her; plan what to do and prepare. Situational awareness is paramount to survival and stress management.

10. Be confident in your ability—be cool, do not act cool. Make yourself believe in your ability to prevail and think that your opponent is not as well trained and prepared as you and will not be able to succeed. Do not be rushed if you can afford it; be calculating and decisive.

11. Your commands—be aware of the commands you give individuals. If you tell them to raise their hands, you will expect this movement and allow them to get ahead of

you if they draw. His calculated action may be quicker than your reflexes; remember action is faster that reaction!

12. Continue your education—learn from those individuals that have been there and done it. You can learn from their mistakes instead of making them yourself and getting the same result.

Hand-and-eye coordination is very important, but not always a natural, instinctive ability of all shooters. It is usually a learned skill obtained by practicing the use of the flash sight picture. The more a shooter practices raising the pistol to eye level and obtaining a flash sight picture, the more natural the relationship between shooter, sights, and target becomes. Eventually, proficiency elevates to a point at which the shooter can accurately engage targets in low-light conditions with little or no use of the sights. Poorly coordinated shooters may achieve proficiency by being closely coached and critiqued. Since pointing the index finger at an object and extending the pistol toward the target are much the same, the combination of the two is natural. Making the shooter aware of this ability and teaching him how to apply it when firing result in success when engaging threat targets in combat situations.

Your choice of weapon, equipment, ammunition, and training will greatly effect your ability to progress and become consistent. With this in mind, you must research what your are training for and acquire the correct equipment. It all must be reliable, not pretty.

The eyes focus instinctively on the center of any object observed. After the object is sighted, the shooter aligns his sights on the center of mass, focuses on the front sight, and applies the proper trigger press straight to the rear. Most crippling and killing hits result from maintaining the focus on the center of mass. As you progress, your sight picture will "soften" and not be as clear as you focus between the front sight and the target; this is very fast and accurate when attained. Both eyes must be used so you are not limited as to your field of view, and they will be open during high-stress situations anyhow—train as you fight.

When a shooter points, he instinctively points at the feature on the object on which his eyes are focused. This point explains why shooters shoot the pistol of their threat: they are focused on their threat's pistol when they fire. Objects like badges assist in giving the opponent a point to look at and use instinctive shooting to hit more accurately than if they tried to use their sights. An impulse from the brain causes the arm and hand to stop when the finger reaches the proper position. When the eyes are shifted to a new object or feature, the finger, hand, and arm also shift to this point. This inherent trait can be used by the shooter to engage targets rapidly and accurately. This instinct is called hand-and-eye-coordination.

Flash sight picture is usually used when engaging a threat at pistol ranges; the shooter has little time to ensure a correct sight picture. The quick kill (or natural point of aim) does not always ensure a first-round hit. A compromise between a correct deliberate sight picture and the quick kill method is known as the flash sight picture. As the shooter raises his pistol to eye level, his point of focus switches from the threat to the front sight, ensuring that the front and rear sight are in proper alignment left and right, but not necessarily up and down. Pressure is applied to the trigger as the front sight is being acquired, and the hammer falls as the flash sight picture is confirmed. Initially, this method should be practiced slowly, gaining speed as proficiency increases. Remember that "slow is smooth and smooth is fast." Take your time and perform the techniques correctly, and speed will show up.

In pistol-distance shooting situations, time is seldom available to apply precisely all of the fundamentals of marksmanship. When a shooter fires a round at a threat, many times he will not know if he hit his target. What the threat is wearing may

FIGURE 8-1   123

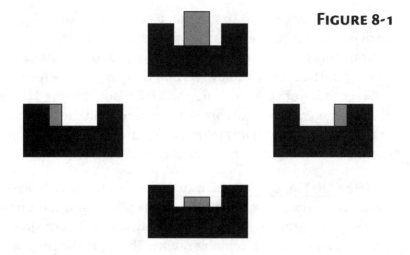

Quick front sight illustrations showing the acceptable variance of the front sight when using a flash sight picture. [This diagram shows flash sight pictures at seven yards. The left and right variations of the front sight will move the impact of the bullet about 2 inches.] The high and low front sight will move the impact of the bullet about 5 inches.

not lead to your seeing a response, and you should be looking at your front sight anyhow. You must "call your shot"—that is, know where your front sight was on the target when the weapon begins recoil. Therefore, you must practice to use a series of shots to incapacitate the threat, not the old two shots and look. You may choose to practice the double tap engagement, two shots in rapid succession "hammers", the controlled pair, two well-aimed shots; or a series of shots until the target has ceased being a threat, or three to five rounds. I will detail the uses of these engagement methods, and you may make your choice.

The <u>double tap</u> is two shots fired with flash sight pictures at fairly close targets. To perform a double tap, you determine that the distance to the target is close enough for your ability to perform a double tap. This distance will change with your ability level, the size of the target, and amount of practice you have performed recently. The shots are fired as soon as you obtain your acceptable flash sight picture. This technique is learned on a range; you must see how you shoot with different sight pictures and figure out how fast your double taps can be to keep the needed accuracy. A good time to practice for is 1.2 – 1.4 seconds from position three on a full silhouette-sized target at seven meters. The shots are not meant to be in the same hole or close to each other; it is to quickly create at least two wound channels in separate parts of the threat.

THE CONTROLLED PAIR: is two well-aimed and well-placed shots at moderate pistol ranges. This distance will also come from your experimenting with different speeds and different sizes of targets to obtain your acceptable results. The key to the controlled pair is that you see three distinctive sight pictures, one before the first shot, one before the second shot, and one after the recoil recovery. This method is the preferred engagement method when you have encountered a need for discriminating shooting, where you must hit only the intended target. These two shots should go exactly where you were aiming.

SHOOT TILL THEY STOP: You may also practice neutralizing your threat with the "shoot till they stop" method of engagement. This method can be three to five shots to the center of mass or the failure-to-stop type drill. The common failure-to-stop-drill is when you engage the threat with two rounds to the center of mass, then one to the center of the head. Other variations are to fire two rounds to the center of mass, then fire two rounds into the hip/pelvic area to break the pelvic girdle in case that the threat is wearing body armor. This approach is more valid than the head shot since the hips are larger than the head and not as likely to be moving as much as the head. These types of engagements may be needed to neutralize the threat from a drug-crazed assailant or a very determined, well-trained and equipped opponent.

In close shooting situations, the threat may be attacking from all sides. The shooter may not have time to change his

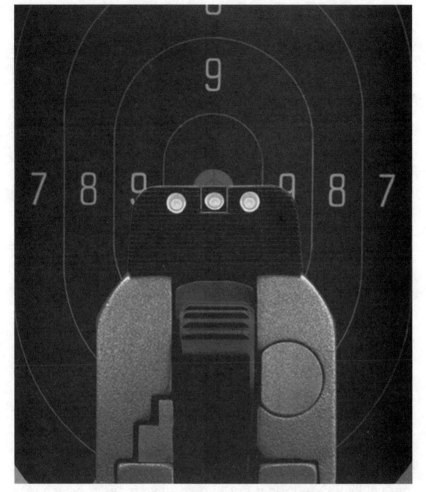

You don't always need a perfect sight picture.

position constantly to adapt to new situations. You should practice traversing from all your shooting positions. Traversing is nothing more that pivoting your upper torso in the direction that is easiest to engage the threat. Some shifting may inevitably occur, but this approach is for extreme situations with survival in mind. If possible, maintain the triangle formed by your two-handed grip with nearly locked elbows to keep your recoil management. By moving your foot, you can quickly pivot to change angles.

COMBAT MARKSMANSHIP

WEAPON RETNTION-

FIGURE 8-2

Weapon retention

Weapon retention is used to fight and/or protect yourself from having your weapon taken away and avoiding contact shots. Your non-firing hand is instrumental to block or grab and pull an attacker depending on his actions. Make sure to roll the pistol out (slide out) so it does not hit you when it cycles, which may induce a malfunction. Ensure you do not shoot your non-firing hand with this technique.

CONTACT SHOOTING: This is the placing of the pistol against the adversary and shooting. This technique will ensure rounds onto meat, but will most likely induce a malfunction. As in Figure 8-2, you should train to keep your pistol back and in a retention position.

MULTIPLE THREATS: You must determine how you are going to handle a multiple-threat situation. There are numerous techniques for this. You must take into account your ability, distance to threats, the size of the threats, actions of the threats, your available cover, and it goes on. I will not advocate any one method as you must decide and live or die by it. You can determine to shoot single shots across the bank of threats and continue back and forth until the threats are neutralized. This technique is based on the idea that multiple wounded threats are at a disadvantage rather than completely stopping one and then working on the next. What works at shooting matches is not always what works for real. Test your theories with Simunitions, and you will see how they are really applied. This single-shot technique can be transformed to two shots, three shots, etc., depending on your decision.

INDEXING: No matter what method of engagement, you must learn to index between the threats by looking to the center of mass of the next target before you bring your weapon to it. This allows you to place precisely your front sight quickly and not overswing past your intended center of mass sight placement. Practice letting the recoil assist you in the movement to the next target. Ensure you have let out just enough slack on the trigger to re-engage the sear and begin the pressure rearward on the trigger so that you may engage the moment your front sight reaches the center of mass.

RHYTHM DRILLS: This drill is used to develop a smooth rhythm, speed, accuracy, proper follow-through, and recovery. Beginners should get a shooting timer for accurate records of progress. Firing a string of shots with a rhythm allows the shooter to measure and improve upon a multiple of tasks. A rhythm to practice for is no more that .06 seconds between the split times between shots. *Example*: The six-shot rhythm drill is designed to develop/test three separate skills. First is the ability to hit the target; second is the ability to acquire the target in a prescribed time frame; and third is the ability to control the trigger squeeze in a smooth, deliberate rhythm. On a larger scale, this drill identifies the shooter's target acquisition and trigger management abilities and also builds both speed and accuracy.

Professional standards place the adversary at about 7 to 10 yards, a composite time of three seconds or less, with no more than .06 seconds between any of the six shots. For example, if the second shot breaks .25 seconds following the first shot, the shot break for each of the following shots must be within .06 seconds of the second shot break. A realistic example follows below:

FIGURE 8-3

Shot Number	Shot Time	Split Time 1-2-3-4-5-6
1	1.05	.30
2	1.35	.31
3	1.66	.33
4	1.99	.35
5	2.34	.30
6	2.64	

In this example, the time requirement of three seconds was met, and there was a range of only .05 seconds between any individual shot. Assuming that each shot was on target, the standard was met. Conversely, if shot number three had a time of 1.73 seconds with a separation of .38 seconds, it would have exceeded the separation break by .02 second (.38 minus .30 = .08), and the shooter would have failed to meet the standard.

To perform a rhythm drill properly with your desired accuracy, you have to command all of the fundamentals mentioned previously. Further development of these skills will increase speed and accuracy. The breaking of the rhythm or the rounds failing to impact in the desired group size will highlight improper grip, stance, lack of proper trigger control, poor recoil management, or improper sight alignment/sight placement. You can make the rhythm drill as many rounds as you would like for practicing the cadence and proper accuracy. Once the rhythm drill is mastered, you can apply it to engaging multiple targets and gradually reduce the amount of time used to complete the drill. A proper rhythm can be more accurate and faster than the standard double tap, double tap, double tap. Get a timer out and try it for yourself.

SHOOTING FROM BEHIND COVER: There are two ways of shooting from behind cover: over it or around it. The preferred technique is to shoot over it. Shooting over cover offers a wider arc of coverage and provides a more stable base if the cover is used as a platform for the weapon. In addition, it doesn't matter whether the shooter is left-handed or right-handed. Remember not to silhouette yourself against a contrasting background because you will be more easily seen. Be back far enough from the cover to fully present without the touching or going past it; economy of effort and economy of motion = efficiency and speed. Refer to figure 8-4A. Remember, the bore is lower than the sights, so take this into account and do not shoot the cover. Refer to figures 8-4 and 8-5.

FIGURE 8-4A

Kneeling position shooting over cover

Kneeling position shooting over cover

Standing position shooting over a vehicle used as cover

FIGURE 8-5B

Standing position shooting over a vehicle used as cover

SHOOTING OVER COVER: (vehicles or a medium to low wall). The shooter should assume a squatting position behind the cover. For lower cover, you may have to assume a kneeling position so as not to expose yourself. The pistol should be presented and ready to shoot. As the shooter comes up from behind the cover, he should expose only enough of himself to make the shot. When shooting over cover, the shooter may use the cover as a shooting platform, provided the pistol does not extend beyond the cover. When using this technique, the shooter should never rest the pistol directly on a hard cover. The bottom of your hands will be padding between the cover and the pistol.

Keep in mind rounds ricochet or travel across hoods of vehicles and walls. In this case, it is better to stay back and give yourself at least 2 to 6 feet of distance from the vehicle or wall. Refer to figures 8-4A and 8-5A.

SHOOTING AROUND COVER: (standing, sitting, kneeling, and prone positions). As in shooting over cover, the shooter should set up as close to the cover as possible when the pistol is mounted in a firing position. This position will expose less of his body to multiple targets as he comes around the cover. Refer to Figure 8-6B. He should shoot the pistol from the primary side (i.e., right-handed going right or left-handed going left) so as to expose less of the body. Refer to Figures 8-6A and 8-7A. If the shooter is not experienced in weak-hand shooting, he should employ a lean technique when going to the non-firing side. When standing or kneeling, the shooter takes a short, quick step out, just far enough to engage the farthest outside target, and then arcs inward, engaging targets as they appear. The technique from the prone position is similar, except that instead of stepping out with the foot, the shooter moves his outside elbow and then rolls to complete his arc. Be aware of how much of your body your are exposing around the cover. Try varying your foot placement with different cover situations to minimize exposure.

Standing use of vertical cover

FIGURE 8-7A

FIGURE 8-7B

Kneeling and prone positions using available cover

WEAPON TRANSITION: You must change to the secondary (pistol) when your primary weapon fails. Pick one of he techniques that will work for you with the equipment and duties you have. If at all posssible and the situation allows it, by all means seek correct cover and perform your weapons transitions.

CLOSE QUARTER BATTLE (CQB) SLING METHOD- The use of a CQB- type sling is very common among operators in military and law enforcement SWAT or direct action-oriented missions. The technique of transitioning to the secondary (pistol) weapon from an empty or malfunctioning primary (rifle or shotgun) is simple as you normally just release the primary. There are variations of this that assist in limiting the movement of the primary as you transition. One of these techniques is to twist the primary with the non-firing hand as you bring it down; with AR-15/M4 and MP5-type weapons, the magazine and sling create tension to hold the weapon against the body. Remember to practice as you fight, and do not wear shorts when doing transition training as when you sear your leg with a hot barrel, you will learn the hard way. Also, some of the mentioned techniques can cause damage to your weapon's finish; this is up to you, but a scratch will not hurt many work weapons, and one day it may save that second you need to survive.

CQB Sling Method

FIGURE 8-8A

FIGURE 8-8B

FIGURE 8-8C

FIGURE 8-8D

FIGURE 8-8E

COMBAT MARKSMANSHIP

Traditional Sling Method

FIGURE 8-9A   **FIGURE 8-9B**   **FIGURE 8-9C**

FIGURE 8-9D   **FIGURE 8-9E**

Notice that both hands are moving at the same time so as not to waste time and effort. Refer to Figures 8-9A through 8-9E. This transition could be used if you are not actively in a fight and need to get your pistol or keep an empty weapon you have more ammunition for and will tactically reload when the situation allows it.

The Lay Down Method

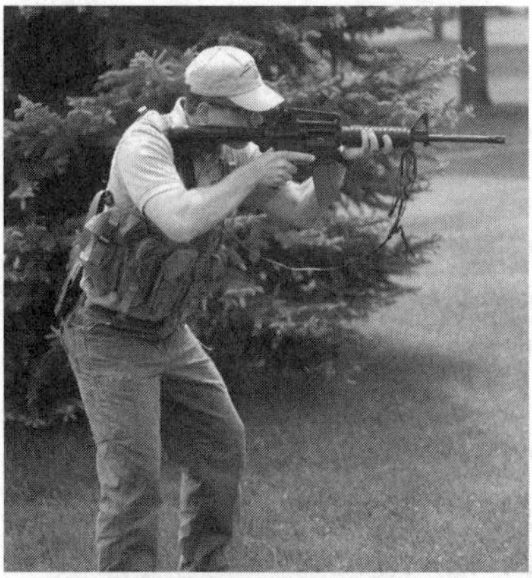

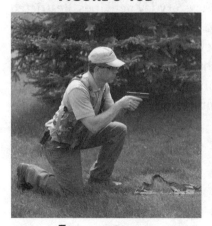

Figure 8-10A

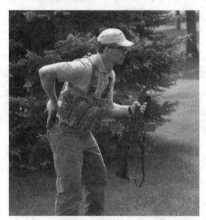

Figure 8-10B

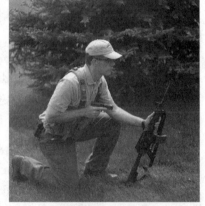

Figure 8-10C

Figure 8-10D

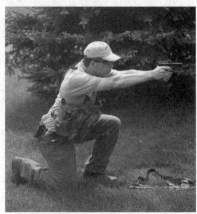

Figure 8-10E

Notice on page 137 that both hands are moving at the same time so as not to waste time and effort. Maintain a grip with the non-firing hand on the primary weapon and begin your draw of your pistol. Refer to Figure 8-10B. Let the buttstock drop from the pocket of the shoulder. Refer to Figure 8-10B. The weapon is now hanging straight down, and when the buttstock is approximately thigh/knee high, let the weapon drop onto the butt and fall forward toward the threat. Refer to Figure 8-10C. Slight pressure is needed to ensure it falls forward. This impact can assist in freeing a stuck casing, making it easier to clear a malfunction, if present, when the engagement is over. As you are ridding yourself of your empty or malfunctioned primary weapon you are going to a kneeling position. Refer to Figure 8-10C. This movement may cause your opponent to lose his sight picture or you could be utilizing available cover to protect yourself during the transition. Remember, you are usually either moving or shooting, rarely at the same time; the situation and your abilities dictates. Continue the engagement as needed from the kneeling position if this is tactically feasible.

USE OF A PROTECTIVE MASK: Shooting with a protective mask or gas mask must be practiced if it is used in your line of work. Your method of engagement and fundamentals should not change. You must have your current prescription optical inserts if you usually wear glasses in your everyday activities. Restricted breathing is the biggest factor to adjust to. And with masks that are not full face, you have a limit on your vision, and this limit must be known and practiced with. Physical activity with the mask on will obviously cause condensation inside the mask to form, so you may need to treat your lenses with an anti-fog substance.

COACHING AND TRAINING PRACTICES

This section will help teach you methods to practice your shooting efficiently and safely. Treat going to the range like going to the gym; pick a focus and then do just that and go home. Progression is a key, but do not progress faster than you can perform correctly. I will begin by emphasizing dry firing practice.

1. **Dry firing:** This is the most effective and cost-efficient type of training. All you need is an empty pistol and a safe place to practice. You may choose to use a small piece of ballistic armor material or a ballistic vest in a room if you want to guarantee that a negligent discharge does not exit the room and injure someone. **Never have loaded magazines or ammunition in the room in which you are dry firing.** Thoroughly check your pistol and magazines to ensure they do not contain live ammunition. You may choose to purchase dummy ammunition or dummy magazines for dry firing. You begin your practice session like any other by having the objectives for your practice. Know what you are going to emphasize in each practice session. Apply the proper techniques and take your time. You can never miss fast enough, so begin slowly. Most modern pistols are not affected by moderate dry firing. A coach, if you have one, is also a valuable dry firing tool to identify what you are doing correctly and incorrectly.

2. **Ball and dummy drill:** For live fire practice. In this method, a coach loads your pistol or magazines for you. He may hand the shooter the loaded weapon or an empty one.

Photo of how to hand a loaded handgun

FIGURE 8-11

When firing a (with an empty chamber or dud round) pistol, the shooter observes that in anticipation of recoil, he is forcing the weapon downward as the hammer falls. Repeated practice of this drill will alleviate recoil anticipation.

3. <u>**Calling the shot:**</u> To call the shot is to state where the bullet should strike the target according to the sight picture at the break of the shot, for example, "to the right," "dead center," etc. If the shooter is not calling the shot correctly in range fire, he is not concentrating on the correct sight alignment. Consequently, he does not know what his sight picture is as he fires. You may also use the clock system for calling the shot. Example: "three inches at three o'clock" is three inches directly to the right of center of mass.

4. <u>**Slow-aimed fire practice:**</u> This exercise is one of the most important for any shooter and is used to evaluate your use and understanding of the fundamentals. This practice is the use of all the shooting fundamentals for each shot fired. Take your time and review the fundamentals before each shot. Do not rush a shot; it is better to start over and do it right than to waste a shot. You should not hold the pistol up at position four for more than five to seven seconds; if you do, just pull back to position three and

then start from there. You can think in your head on what you personally have to concentrate. Some say "front sight, press" until the pistol fires to concentrate on their sight picture and trigger control. Remember that the proper trigger control allows the hammer to fall without the front sight moving. Some movement is acceptable, but practice to minimize it. And remember to call the shot after each shot. To build speed, you need to perform the actions in a technically correct manner and focus on minimizing movements (economy of motion and effort = speed). You should build speed by sometimes speeding up to miss 30%, then slowing back down to 100% hits, a push/pull method.

5. **Air pistols:** You may use air pistols to provide realistic low-cost training. The fundamentals all still apply, just on a different type of pistol. Remember the safety considerations also apply.

6. **Timers:** An affordable but dependable shooting timer cannot be overstated. Used properly, it will give you a true figure to calculate your progress. The basic timer can track your time of shots and the split time between shots. Refer to Figure 8-12.

Competition Electronics Pocket Pro Timer

FIGURE 8-12

Shooting chart for the right-handed shooter
(Left-handed shooters use a mirror image to diagnose)

Breaking wrist down.
Not concentrating on the front sight
(front sight low).
Anticipating recoil and jerking trigger.

Applying too much or too little finger to trigger
Improper placement of pistol in hand.

Applying strong thumb pressure.
Anticipating recoil (pulling the trigger at angle).

Jerking the trigger (snatching).
Canting the weapon to the left and allowing the
barrel to drop.

Squeezing the whole hand with the trigger
squeeze.
Slack wrist.
Jerking the trigger.

No specific error; all prerequisites for a clean
shot are lacking.
Lack of front sight focus.

Not leveling the front sight in rear sight.
Unsteady weapons platform.

Not centering the front sight in the rear sight
notch.
Unsteady weapons platform or unequal grip
pressure.

Pulling back on the weapon when firing.
Breaking of the wrist (heeling).
Not concentrating on the sight alignment (front
sight too high/looking over the top of the rear sight).

SHOOTING DRILLS FOR PRACTICE
Presented in the order of progression-

1. **DRY FIRING PRACTICE:** The use of dummy cartridges, dummy weapons, and/or dummy magazines to practice new techniques or for warm-up exercises.

2. **BALL-AND-DUMMY DRILL:** The practice technique of loading a dummy round into the chamber or within a loaded magazine by the coach so the shooter will see if they are performing proper fundamentals. If they anticipate the blast or recoil, they will pull the pistol and interrupt sight placement.

3. **SLOW-AIMED FIRE:** Fundamental marksmanship practice to utilize all the fundamentals and have the bullet go where desired by the shooter.

4. **PRESENTATION POSITION THREE TO FOUR DRILL:** This drill is essential to learn to break the shot at the point of full extension

and hit your desired target. This drill must be mastered to progress in speed or accuracy with whatever type of automatic pistol you use.

5. **CONTROLLED PAIRS:** The practice of attaining two well-aimed and well-placed shots from the holster or position three to build confidence or practice shots of distance and/or small targets.

6. **DOUBLE TAPS:** Practicing to attain the rapid secession of shots and maintain your desired accuracy. Emphasize proper focus on the sights and minimal movement of the trigger.

7. **DRAWING FROM A HOLSTER:** The proper four-step draw sequence is one of the foundations for further progress. This techniques must be learned correctly and remain consistent for further progress.

8. **RHYTHM DRILL:** This drill is to practice trigger control and recoil management and leads to speeding up on multiple targets by smoothing out a cadence of shots. They must be a set of shots at a steady rhythm, depending on the designated target or targets.

9. **KNEELING DRILL:** Practicing how you will kneel for various situations and practicing with the equipment used.

10. **PRONE DRILL:** Practicing how you will use the prone position for various situations and practicing with the equipment to be used.

11. **SUPINE DRILL:** Practicing how you will use the supine position for various situations and practicing with the equipment used. Remember where your feet are!

12. **HIGH BARRICADE:** A drill utilizing a high horizontal barricade to let you practice setting up your standing position and shooting over it or around it.

13. **Low barricade:** A drill utilizing a low horizontal barricade to let you practice setting up your position and shooting over it from the prone, sitting, and/or kneeling positions around it.

14. **Turning left/right drill:** These drills are designed to allow you to practice how much movement is needed and the specifics of getting to the oblique to make the shot.

15. **Turning about drill:** This drill is designed to allow you to practice how much movement is needed and the specifics of getting to the rear to make the shot. Also called the PRA drill—the perceiving of a threat, recognition of a threat, and the acquiring of the threat with the pistol.

16. **Weapon retention:** This drill is designed to allow you to become more familiar and comfortable firing from position two of the draw.

17. **Move forward, stop, shoot whistle drill:** This drill is used to get you shooting at someone else's command, forcing you to be comfortable in shooting during movement.

18. **Move forward and shoot whistle drill:** This drill is used to get you shooting at someone else's command, forcing you to be comfortable in shooting during movement.

19. **Strong-hand draw drill:** This drill is used to build your confidence in shooting with only your strong-hand when your non-firing arm is injured or unusable.

20. **Weak-hand draw drill:** This drill is used to build your confidence in shooting with only your non-firing (weak) hand when your dominant firing arm is injured or unusable.

21. **Shooting from a vehicle:** This drill is used to familiarize the shooter with shooting out of a vehicle effectively. You can always get a new windshield, but not a new life.

22. **SHOOTING INTO A VEHICLE:** This drill familiarizes the shooter with how to shoot effectively a threat in a vehicle.

23. **SHOOTING WHILE WOUNDED, STRONG-HAND RELOAD:** This drill is used to build your confidence in reloading with only your strong hand when you non-firing arm is injured or unusable.

24. **SHOOTING WHILE WOUNDED, WEAK-HAND RELOAD:** This drill is used to build your confidence in reloading with only your weak hand when your firing (dominant) arm is injured or unusable.

25. **SHOOTING WHILE WOUNDED, STRONG-HAND MALFUNCTIONS:** This drill is used to build your confidence in correcting malfunctions with only your strong hand when you non-firing arm is injured or unusable.

26. **SHOOTING WHILE WOUNDED, WEAK-HAND MALFUNCTIONS:** This drill is used to build your confidence in correcting malfunctions with only your non-dominant (weak) hand when your firing arm is injured or unusable.

Important Notes:

- Keep finger off the trigger until on target and ready to engage.
- Maintain control—know where it is pointed at all times.
- Only go as fast as your ability allows and attain a 100 percent hit standard for the combat mindset when your life depends upon it.
- Slow is smooth and smooth is fast. Get faster by eliminating excess actions/movements, not just by speeding up.
- Remember to shoot correctly and not to shoot excessive amounts. 350 rounds a day are my maximum for a good training day.
- Push yourself to missing up to 30 percent, then slow back to 100 percent hits into your acceptable target size—improve speed and accuracy.
- Treat range practice like going to the gym—plan your session, keep records, use coaches (that know what they are talking about), and leave when the results are attained—focus on what you are wanting to improve.
- Finish range sessions with a drill you do well to build/ maintain confidence.
- Consistent, proper procedures and proper training will build confidence, speed and accuracy.

PISTOL
PROFILE

KIMBER
MODEL: TACTICAL PRO II

Caliber	Barrel Length	Overall Length	Nom. Weight	Magazine Capacity
9mm	4 "	7.7 "	1 lbs. 13 oz.	7
.45 ACP	4 "	7.7 "	1 lbs. 13 oz.	7

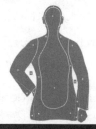

CHAPTER NINE

SHOOTING WHILE WOUNDED

The most advanced pistolcraft is conducting shooting-while-wounded drills with both the strong and weak sides. These techniques will save your life when the chips are down. The key is never to quit the fight. If you have to head butt the aggressor to death, then this is what you will have to do. Your adrenaline will allow you to do amazing acts in the worst situations, so use it to save your life or others' lives.

NOTE: These techniques are dangerous if practiced incorrectly, so be very aware of the details of these techniques. If you doubt your ability to conduct these drills, seek professional instruction so you may learn them safely.

You should practice as if you have been wounded before you could draw your pistol and after you have drawn your pistol with both your strong and weak hands. Holster selection and placement come into play, as some body types are more advantageous than others. You will still have to tailor these techniques so they work for

you, but remember to watch your muzzle direction and keep the finger off the trigger when not on target and willing to engage.

Both kneeling and standing positions are detailed. Kneeling is preferred if tactically feasible due to the low center of gravity; you are a smaller target and close to the ground if you drop something.

FIGURE 9-1

I will begin explaining shooting while wounded with the non-firing hand being wounded from some form of injury, whether from gunshots or a car accident. Think about how your non-firing hand is most likely to be wounded as your attacker is shooting center of mass, and if you are at full presentation, this is where your arms are. This technique is one of the simplest since you are used to drawing with just your strong-hand, but your presentation from position three to position four is different. I will begin with standing while shooting with the strong hand and progress into magazine changes and malfunction correction drills.

STEP ONE: As you draw your pistol with your strong hand, bring your wounded arm to the centerline of your chest as best you can (Figure 9-1). This position helps with balance and recoil management.

STEP TWO: As you present your pistol towards the threat, step your firing foot towards the threat and present a side profile to your threat. This step will allow the recoil to come through your arm to your upper torso, and you will be better able to handle the pistol while shooting. Lean slightly forward from the hips.

STEP THREE: At full presentation, slightly cant your pistol to the left (no more than 45 degrees) to allow you to tighten your wrist and use the larger muscles of your forearm to force the recoil through your arm to your torso (Figure 9-9). Align the sights and press the trigger straight to the rear.

Effective use of cover is soemthing that must be practiced.

STRONG-HAND SHOOTING WHILE WOUNDED, MAGAZINE CHANGE-

KNEELING

| FIGURE 9-2A | FIGURE 9-2B |

STEP ONE: Go to a two-knee kneeling position. As you go down, you can depress the magazine release to drop the magazine or turn the pistol upside down and pinch the pistol with your knees (Figure 9-2A). While pinching the pistol with your knees, depress the magazine release and remove the used magazine. Drop that magazine and locate the fresh magazine in your magazine pouch by reaching across your body to your magazine pouch (Figure 9-2B).

NOTE: Caution—be careful not to let the muzzle impact into the ground as it may cause an obstruction in soft dirt/sand/mud in the muzzle.

STEP TWO: Properly insert and seat the fresh magazine with the palm of your hand (Figure 9-3B). Only glance at your magazine well as you begin to put the magazine in it; then refocus on the threat (Figure 9-3A).

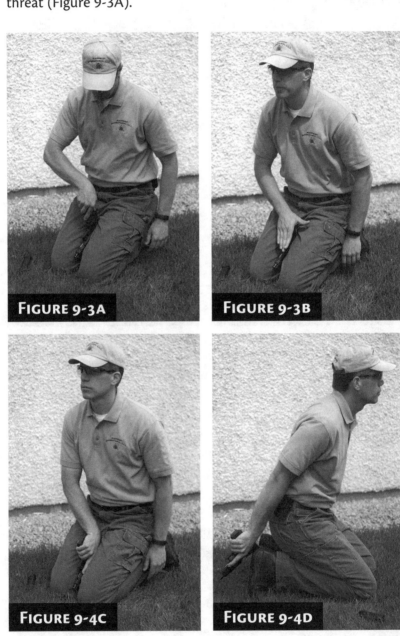

FIGURE 9-3A

FIGURE 9-3B

FIGURE 9-4C

FIGURE 9-4D

STEP THREE: Regrip the pistol (Figure 9-4a). If the slide is locked to the rear, you only have to release the slide with the slide release using your thumb. If the pistol's slide is closed, use the technique of cycling the slide by hooking the rear sight on your boot, belt, holster, or whatever is available (Figure 9-4b). Once the rear sight is hooked, force the pistol down and away to cycle the action and ensure that clothing or equipment doesn't interfere.

FIGURE 9-5

STEP FOUR: Continue the engagement as the situation dictates (Figure 9-5). Remember to slightly cant the pistol to the left to tighten up your arm to allow for greater recoil management or straight up as normally fired.

STRONG-HAND SHOOTING WHILE WOUNDED MAGAZINE CHANGE-

STANDING

FIGURE 9-6

STEP ONE: Whether you are changing your magazine because it is empty or you want to recharge the pistol with a fresh one in the standing position, remember to seek protective cover, not just concealment. Insert the pistol into your holster and remove the magazine and put it in a pocket; if empty, discard it (Figure 9-6). Maintain your focus to the threat are.

FIGURE 9-7A   **FIGURE 9-7B**   **FIGURE 9-7C**

STEP TWO: With the strong arm, remove a fresh magazine from your magazine pouch and insert it into the magazine well. Utilize the proper grip on the magazine as described earlier, index finger extended on the front of the magazine and pinched by the thumb and middle finger (Figure 9-7A). You may have to glance quickly at the magazine well to ensure the magazine goes in the first time attempted (Figure 9-7B). Once the magazine is in the magazine well, shift your focus back to the threat area and firmly seat the magazine to ensure it is locked (Figure 9-7C).

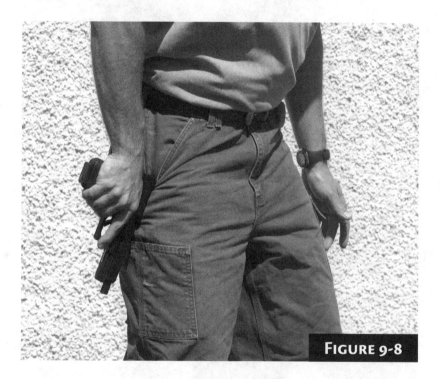

FIGURE 9-8

STEP THREE: If the slide is forward, you will use whatever you have on you or near you to rack the slide to the rear to cycle the next round. You can use your belt, holster, corner of a wall or door, or a pocket (Figure 9-8). If the slide is already locked back, you only have to press down the slide release with the strong-hand thumb.

STEP FOUR: Continue to fight (Figure 9-9).

FIGURE 9-9

STRONG-HAND SHOOTING WHILE WOUNDED-

MALFUNCTIONS: Correcting malfunctions should be conducted from the two-knee kneeling position if tactically feasible. This lowering of the body helps with balance when you are under great stress and allows you to pick up easily anything from the ground if dropped accidentally. It is very important to seek bulletproof cover while correcting malfunctions with one hand. The practice of these malfunction drills is essential to correct the malfunction safely when you have the disadvantage of using just one arm. The symptoms of the malfunction are the same as previously covered for each type of malfunction.

NOTE: All actions with the pistol except the actual shooting are performed with the finger off the trigger; this point is very important to prevent negligent discharges while operating.

KNEELING

FAILURE TO FIRE- TYPE I: Slide is forward on an empty chamber or the pistol was loaded with a dud round. The correction is the same as with two hands, except you are using just the good arm.

FIGURE 9-10

STEP ONE: Once you have detected a failure to fire, you must immediately remove your finger from the trigger guard. **SLAP** the butt of the pistol on your thigh to seat the magazine positively (Figure 9-10).

FIGURE 9-11

STEP TWO: RACK the slide to the rear and allow it to shut by its own spring tension. You can also force the slide to the rear by hooking the front sight of the pistol on your belt, holster, boot, or pocket (Figure 9-11). Be very aware of your muzzle direction and ensure that your finger is off the trigger. Since this is a critical act, you may have to shift focus to ensure your slide is correctly placed. Immediately regain focus toward the threat once the sight is placed correctly.

FIGURE 9-12

STEP THREE: READY, continue the engagement as the situation dictates (Figure 9-12).

FAILURE TO FIRE- TYPE I: Slide is forward on an empty chamber or the pistol was loaded with a dud round. The correction is the same as with two hands, except you are using just the good arm.

FIGURE 9-13

STEP ONE: Once you drop the hammer on an empty chamber or on a dud round, immediately remove your finger from the trigger and the trigger guard. **SLAP** the magazine into the magazine well by firmly seating the butt of the pistol on your thigh (Figure 9-3).

STEP TWO: RACK the slide to the rear by hooking your rear sight on your belt, holster, pocket, or whatever you have available. Since this is a critical act, you may have to shift focus to ensure your slide is correctly placed (Figure 9-14). Immediately regain focus toward the threat once the sight is placed correctly.

FIGURE 9-14

FIGURE 9-15A

FIGURE 9-15B

STEP THREE: READY, continue the engagement as the situation dictates (Figure 9-15A&B).

FAILURE TO EJECT- TYPE II: The empty casing is not fully ejected and is pinched in the slide. This corrective action is as simple as with two hands.

STANDING AND KNEELING MAY BE DONE IN THE SAME WAY.

FIGURE 9-16A   FIGURE 9-16B

STEP ONE: Once you have identified that you have a stovepipe malfunction, immediately remove your finger from the trigger guard. Using some part of your belt kit or boot, rest the protruding casing against it and vigorously push against the casing and force it to be released by the slide (Figures 9-16A and 9-16B). Ensure you do not fully work the slide to the rear as this may induce a double feed-Type III malfuntion.

SHOOTING WOUNDED

FIGURE 9-17

STEP TWO: Continue the engagement as the situation dictates. Refer to Figure 9-17.

FAILURE TO EXTRACT- TYPE III: The spent casing is not extracted from the chamber and the next loaded round is being forced in behind it. Standing or kneeling uses essentially the same correction.

FIGURE 9-18

FIGURE 9-19

STEP ONE: Once you have identified a double-feed malfunction, immediately remove your finger from within the trigger guard. Refer to Figure 9-18. Lock the slide to the rear by moving the pistol in your hand so you can engage the slide release with your thumb. While pushing up on the slide release with your thumb, hook the rear sight on your belt kit or boot and force the slide to the rear (Figure 9-19). You may have to shift your focus to ensure you lock the slide to the rear quickly.

STEP TWO: Remove the magazine by pushing the magazine release button with your thumb (Figure 9-20) and work the action at least three times to ensure the stuck casing has been ejected (Figure 9-21). Use your boot or belt to hook your rear sight onto to cycle the pistol.

FIGURE 9-20

FIGURE 9-21

FIGURE 9-22A

FIGURE 9-22B

STEP THREE: Place the pistol muzzle down between your knees, remove a fresh magazine (if not previously done), and then properly insert and seat the fresh magazine (Figures 9-22A through 9-22C). Since this is a critical act, you may have to shift focus to ensure your magazine is inserted into the magazine well correctly.

FIGURE 9-22C

Immediately regain focus toward the threat once the magazine is started into the magazine well.

STEP FOUR: Cycle a round into the chamber by once again hooking the rear sight on your boot, belt, or whatever you have that will do it and force the slide to the rear and allow it to return by its own spring tension (Figure 9-23).

FIGURE 9-23

STEP FIVE: Continue the engagement (Figure 9-24). Remember to cant the pistol no more than 45 degrees to the left to use the stronger muscles in your forearm to tame the recoil or straight up as normally fired.

FIGURE 9-24

WEAK-HAND SHOOTING WHILE WOUNDED

Weak-hand shooting while wounded is the most difficult technique for most to learn. Careful study and proper practice will help you perfect this valuable training. The first problem you will encounter while shooting with your non-firing hand is getting to your pistol, which is on your strong side. Below are some different techniques you may study to see what works for you and your body style.

THE DRAW

FIGURE 9-25A   **FIGURE 9-25B**   **FIGURE 9-25C**

You may be able to draw your pistol by pulling your gunbelt around to your non-firing side so you can reach your pistol (Figures 9-25A throug 9-25C).

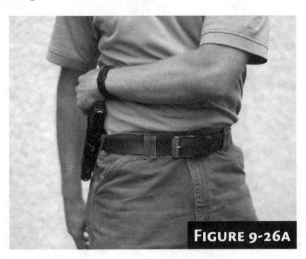

FIGURE 9-26A

FIGURE 9-26B

You may be able to reach around your front to turn the pistol in your holster and get the proper grip and draw the pistol (Figures 9-26a and 926b).

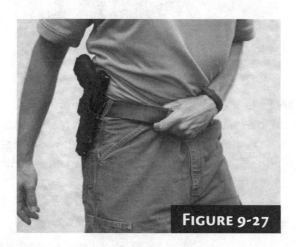

FIGURE 9-27

You may have to pull your gunbelt toward your non-firing side to assist you in drawing your pistol with your non-firing hand (Figure 9-27).

SHOOTING WOUNDED

WEAK-HAND SHOOTING WHILE WOUNDED, MAGAZINE CHANGE

KNEELING

FIGURE 9-28

STEP ONE: Once you have decided to perform a non-firing hand magazine change, you can either pinch the pistol muzzle down between your knees or pinch it between your thigh and calf muscle (Figure 9-28). Depress the magazine release and remove the magazine.

FIGURE 9-29A   **FIGURE 9-29B**   **FIGURE 9-29C**

STEP TWO: Remove a fresh magazine from your magazine pouch, properly insert it into the magazine well, and firmly seat it with the heel of your hand (Figures 9-29A throgh 9-29C).

FIGURE 9-30

FIGURE 9-31

STEP THREE: If the slide is locked to the rear, you must simply shut it by pushing down with your index finger on the slide release to allow it to shut (Figure 9-30). If it is closed, you must rack the slide, keeping your finger off the trigger and outside the trigger guard, and using your belt, boot, or whatever is available (Figure 9-31).

FIGURE 9-32

STEP FOUR: Continue the engagement as the situation dictates (Figure 9-32).

WEAK-HAND SHOOTING WHILE WOUNDED, MAGAZINE CHANGE

STANDING

FIGURE 9-33   FIGURE 9-34

STEP ONE: Once you have decided to perform a non-firing hand reload while standing, you need to seek protective cover. You must release the magazine by pushing on the magazine release with your non-firing hand index finger (Figure 9-33). If the magazine does not fall out of the magazine well, you will have to strip it with your pocket or your gunbelt (Figure 9-34).

FIGURE 9-35A   FIGURE 9-35B   FIGURE 9-35C

STEP TWO: Either pinch the pistol between your knees or replace it in the holster backwards and insert the fresh magazine from your magazine pouch. Be sure to seat the magazine firmly to ensure it is locked in place (Figures 9-35A through 9-35C).

FIGURE 9-36

STEP THREE: Now you must load the chamber by shutting the slide if it is locked to the rear, and this step is done by pushing down on the slide release with your non-firing hand index finger. If the slide is shut, you must rack the slide with your belt, pant pocket, or whatever you have available (Figure 9-36).

FIGURE 9-37

STEP FOUR: Continue the engagement as the situation dictates (Figure 9-37).

WEAK-HAND SHOOTING WHILE WOUNDED, MALFUNCTIONS

FAILURE TO FIRE-TYPE I- Both standing and kneeling are very similar (Figures 9-38 through 9-40).

FAILURE TO EJECT- TYPE II- The corrective action for the stovepipe-type malfunction is the same as for the strong-hand technique, but it is performed with the non-firing hand.

FIGURE 9-38　　**FIGURE 9-39**　　　**FIGURE 9-40**

FAILURE TO EXTRACT- TYPE III- The spent casing is not extracted from the chamber, and the next loaded round is being forced in behind it. Standing or kneeling uses essentially the same correction. Employ the strong-hand technique, except you must practice locking the slide to the rear by pushing up the slide release with the trigger finger. Refer to strong-hand figures 9-18 through 9-24.

STEP ONE: Once you have identified a double-feed malfunction, immediately remove your finger from within the trigger guard. Lock the slide to the rear by moving the pistol in your hand so you can engage the slide release with your trigger finger. While pushing up on the slide release with your trigger finger, hook the rear sight on your belt kit or boot and force the slide to the rear.

STEP TWO: Remove the magazine by pushing the magazine release button with your trigger finger and work the action at least three times to ensure the stuck casing has been ejected. Hook your rear sight onto your boot or belt to cycle the pistol.

STEP THREE: Place the pistol muzzle down between your knees, remove a fresh magazine, and properly insert and seat the fresh magazine.

STEP FOUR: Cycle a round into the chamber by once again hooking the rear sight on your boot, belt, or whatever you have that will do it and force the slide to the rear and allow it to return by its own spring tension.

STEP FIVE: Continue the engagement. Remember to cant the pistol no more than 45 degrees to the left to use the stronger muscles in your forearm to tame the recoil.

PICKING UP YOUR FALLEN PISTOL- During a gunfight where you have sustained injuries to one or both of your arms, you will probably need to pick up your pistol to continue the fight. This action sounds simple, but stress makes the simplest tasks more difficult. These techniques are meant to allow you to train as you fight, so you should practice these as detailed below.

If the butt of the pistol is facing your firing side, you must simply lift up the slide with the non-firing hand as you begin to form your strong-hand grip and roll the pistol into your hand (Figures 9-41A and 9-41B). If the butt is facing your non-firing side, simply roll the butt across so it is facing the other way and do as described above. Consistency will build confidence, speed, and accuracy.

FIGURE 9-41A

FIGURE 9-41B

FIGURE 9-42

FIGURE 9-43

Picking up a pistol with only your firing hand when the grip is facing your firing side (Figure 9-42) and away from your non-firing side (Figure 9-43).

Picking up with your non-firing hand when the grip is away from your firing side (Figure 9-44).

FIGURE 9-44   **FIGURE 9-45**

STEP ONE- Reach across the pistol so you can lift up the butt of it (Figure 9-44).
STEP TWO- As you roll it over to your non-firing side, begin to form your one-handed grip (Figure 9-45).

FIGURE 9-46   **FIGURE 9-47**

STEP THREE- Once you have fully rolled the pistol over and you have your correct one-handed grip, you can continue the engagement (Figures 9-46 and 9-47).

PISTOL PROFILE

GLOCK
MODEL: 35

Caliber	Barrel Length	Overall Length	Nom. Weight	Magazine Capacity
.40	5.32"	8.15"	24.52 oz.	10

CHAPTER TEN

LOW-LIGHT SHOOTING

The use of white lights to aid your shooting in low-light situations is not to be understated. This section is not called night shooting as others describe shooting with white light aids since in a basement at noon, it may be just as dark as at midnight; these situations are low light. You can encounter many situations where a white visible light source, a flashlight, can greatly increase your chance of survival.

The advantages are that white light sources are available to all, inexpensive, and easily maintained. You need not buy the biggest and best light, but you must buy a dependable one and have it with you when you need it.

Check out WWW.BHIGEAR.COM for quality lights and accessories. White lights offer the quickest means of identifying targets and searching areas. The shooter uses his pistol sights just as he does in daylight situations. Beware that the light can compromise your location if you are using it near an undetected threat. Also, it may be accidentally activated and give away your position at an inappropriate time.

You must decide what type of light you are going to use and decide when you are going to use it. Many companies are now adding a flashlight pouch on their magazine pouches as the importance of such items is now being rediscovered. I will discuss the different shooting techniques with flashlights, and you may tailor them to the flashlight and technique you like. You may also decide about the light types that mount onto your pistol. This light is by far the most useful in low-light shooting situations. Quality counts for the pistol-mounted lights since they must stay securely mounted and the bulb must withstand the repeated recoil or firing.

Tritium sights are available in many types and prices. They are good for low-light shooting when your situation allows you to identify your threat and not compromise your location by using a white light. The most common sight configuration is the three tritium dots; various colors are also available. Remember, when you are deciding which sight to purchase, you get what you pay for. Gunsmith installation may be necessary on some pistols.

FIGURE 10-1

Glock 23 with M3 Laser/Illuminator from Streamlight

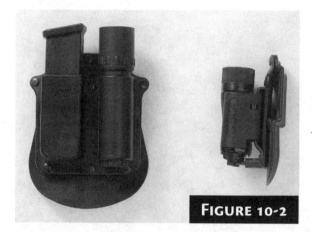

*Fobus Magazine/
Sunfire 6P Combo
pouch and M3/6
carrier*

FIGURE 10-2

Various methods you can use-

FIGURE 10-4

Crossed wrist technique

1. **Crossed wrist technique**- (Also known as the Harries Technique) Hold the flashlight in the non-firing hand. Cross the hand with the flashlight under the firing hand at the wrist and control the light on/off switch with a finger or thumb of the non-firing hand (Figure 10-4).

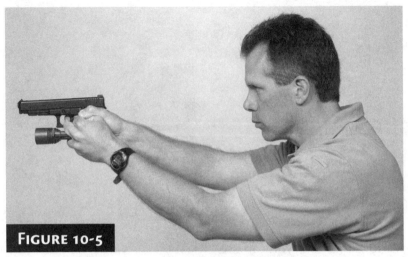

FIGURE 10-5

Knuckle-to-Knuckle technique

FIGURE 10-6

Knuckle-to-Knuckle technique close-up

2. **Knuckle-to-knuckle technique**- Hold the flashlight in the non-firing hand parallel to the firing hand. The knuckles of the second joint of the fingers on the non-firing hand should contact the knuckles of the second joint on the firing hand (Figure 10-5). Above are two variations of holding the light, mostly used when the light needs to be constantly on.

Offset technique

3. __The offset method__- With the non-firing hand, form a grip on the light body with the four fingers and use them to activate lights with switches on the rear (Figure 10-7). The thumb or the forefinger may control the on/off switch. This method is used if you do not want to disclose your exact location while using the white light.

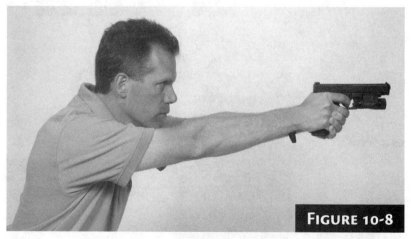

Glock with a Streamlight M3

4. __Weapon mounted light__- Some weapons are designed to have lights mounted on them (Figure 10-8). These are most preferred

for precise tactical shooting and general use, and since you use your normal grip, it is very accurate and quick. Many are now available that quickly attach and detach, which allows the pistols with accessory rails such as the Glock with a Streamlight M6 tactical light (Figure 10-1).

5. **Flashlight on the primary weapon technique**- This technique is used when the primary weapon (rifle or shotgun) has a light source mounted on it. If the weapon malfunctions, the light source can still be used. Simply support the weapon with the non-firing arm (Figures 10-9A and 10-9B). Aim the light source/primary weapon at the target and fire the secondary weapon (pistol) using the single-hand firing technique.

Photos of a primary weapon light being used with pistol

FIGURE 10-9A

FIGURE 10-9B

Low-light considertions-

Light usage during malfunctions and reloads-

Most operators carry a multitude of lights to serve different purposes, and if you can only carry one, make sure it works with all your potential activities. Using handheld lights during malfunction corrections and reloads has to be practiced as you only have two hands. The most common method is to place the flashlight under you firing side armpit. This allows you to use your empty non-firing hand to correct the malfunction and/or reload the pistol. Obviously, if you do not need the light on to correct the malfunction or reload, have it off so you do not give away your location. Once your pistol is ready you can continue with your situation as you decided.

Light usage while shooting while wounded-

If anything can get more complicated, it would be shooting with a light not attached to your weapon while you are wounded. This should help you decide to get some type of weapon mounted light as you will have the rest of your life (though it may be short?) to work with the flashlight and pistol into a winning combination.

Remember that if you are working with others in a situation where white lights are used, you do not all have to turn your lights on. Use only the amount of light needed to accomplish the given task.

Always plan to have extra batteries and bulbs for replacing when needed to keep the light operational.

Lights can be used to temporarily disorient or blind potential threats when they are first encountered, or as a control technique.

When shooting with a light in low-light, you will notice that your shot groups will be tighter. You have fewer destractions, and the sights are silhouetted on the target from the light.

You need not buy the biggest and best light, but you must buy a dependable one and have it with you when you need it.

Focus your beam if you have an adjustable head on your flashlight. Too wide a beam can sometimes prevent you from seeing details as clearly as possible.

To search rooms, you can aim the center of the beam at the baseboard/floor or the wall/ceiling; this will maximize the illuminated area.

When searching use short, sweeping scans, and once you have a quick look, turn off the light and move your position before continuing. Remember, you lose your night vision as soon as you flash, and it takes time to readjust to the level of ambient light. One technique to use is to close your dominant eye to save its night vision; situation dictates. If you must shoot, you can quickly open your dominant eye and engage the threat.

You can practice with a partner to use a "volley fire" (one uses his/her light, then turns it off and the other uses his/hers) method of searching to confuse and yet still effectively search. You can also just use one light so the other operator is not compromising his position.

Have your weapon ready when you do turn your light on so you can deal with what you see as soon as possible. You should not be suprised to find what you are actually looking for; mentally prepare for the discovery of what you are searching for so you can quickly accomplish the mission.

Remember that the brightness of your pistol's muzzle flash and those of others that are near by will be affected by the environmental factors, the barrel length, and types and amount of powder used. Test and familiarize yourself and your team with the weapons you use so you are not suprised by these effects.

You will sacrifice your element of surprise with white light and might want to test and evaluate an infrared (IR) light option utilizing night vision goggles and IR flashlights. Also, you may utilize an IR light beam as an aiming point designator.

Know the moans and groans of your pistol because you can feel malfunctions in low-light as you most likely will not see the malfunction of your pistol. Stress the learning of the symptoms of the different malfunctions, their feels and sounds, to know when to conduct the correct malfunction corrective action. As mentioned previously, you can place the flashlight under your firing side armpit. You may plan a code word with your partners to communicate to them that you are out of the fight with a malfunction. Obviously, seek cover if available and the situation allows it. Once the problem is identified, turn off your light and fix it.

Darkness can be concealment but is definitely not cover, so plan accordingly. Low-light environments only complicate operations so practice these methods often to become more comfortable and competent at operating in this situation.

PISTOL
PROFILE

HK
HECKLER & KOCH
MODEL: USP TACTICAL

Caliber	Barrel Length	Overall Length	Nom. Weight	Magazine Capacity
.40 S&W	6.34"	8.64"	1.90 lb	13
.45 ACP	6.34"	8.64"	1.90 lb	12

CHAPTER ELEVEN

LEFT HAND-DOMINANT SHOOTER

*T*his chapter was included because few references exist for the specific training of left hand-dominant shooters. Tom Bullins of Trigger Time Valley, a left-handed firearms instructor and shooter, has compiled this chapter for your education. This information will also help right hand-dominant shooters with their weak-hand shooting. Very few left-handed firearms instructors correctly teach shooting. Most left-handed shooters are taught to shoot right handed in the armed forces; also note that most holsters for militaries are right-handed. When Tom was in the Marine Corps, he was charged with protecting some of the nation's most important assets and was forced to use a right-hand holster and a 1911A1 with no ambidextrous safety. He had to put a lot of thought and practice into drawing and firing with this configuration. He noted during training courses that right-handed instructors fail to teach left-handed shooters the correct way to work their pistols.

Considerations since most pistols are made with right-handed shooters in mind:

- The magazine release and the slide release are on the wrong side.
- The decock lever is usually not in an easily reached location.
- The magazine release button may be depressed if you are using an inside-the-pants holster for concealed carry.
- The safety can accidently be disengaged when carrying the weapon in right-handed holsters.
- Adding extensions to magazine releases and slide releases should be avoided; certain extended slide stops do work well on Glocks.
- Utilizing the "slingshot" method to release the slide is a good idea for left-handed shooters when properly done. Maintain the muzzle to threat and pivot the pistol on its bore to the non-firing hand to slingshot the slide. The advantage to the left handed shooter is that they will not have to regrip the pistol with the firing hand, thus saving time reacquiring the grip and target.
- The magazine release can be depressed by using the trigger finger, and using the trigger finger also may actuate some slide releases.

Cross eye-dominant shooter considerations—when the shooter is left handed, but right-eye dominant:

- Move the pistol under your dominant eye or make a small movement of the head to the pistol; make sure the dominant eye is behind the sights of the pistol. This will speed up sight acquisition and increase accuracy.
- Some shooters may have to shut their non-dominant eye to get the correct sight alignment and sight placement.

APPENDIX A

SHOOTING SCHOOLS

Absolute Tactical Training
2573 Market St.
San Diego, California 92102
619-858-5832
FAX: 619-692-9408
http://www.absolutetacticaltraining.com
Keiko Arroyo, Chief Instructor

Academy of Personal Protection and Security
336 Hill Ave.
Suite 102
Nashville, Tennessee 37210
615-360-6002
FAX: 615-366-7374
http://www.appstraining.com
J. Buford Tune, Director

Advanced Training Assoc.
6136 Mission Gorge Rd #220
San Diego, CA 92120
619-644-1342
Kurt Sawatzky and Lin Henry, Instructors

Advanced Tactical Technologies Inc.
PO Box 51404
Phoenix, AZ 85076
602-706-8010

Blackheart International, LLC
112 Wood Street
Philippi, WV 26416
304-457-1280
FAX: 304-457-1281
support@bhigear.com
http://www.bhigear.com
Erik Lawrence, Training Director / Author

Advanced Weapons and Tactics
PO Box 6258
Napa, CA 94581
707-253-8926
FAX: 707-253-8927
http://www.awt-co.com
Walt Marshall, Instructor

Allsafe Defense Systems
1026 N. Tustin Ave.
Orange, CA 92867-5958
714-744-4485
http://www.allsafedefense.com
T.J. Johnston, Instructor

American Pistol & Rifle Association
(APRA members only)
Firearms Academy Staff
Box USA
Benton, TN 37307
615-338-2328

American Shooting Academy
PO Box 54233
Phoenix, AZ 85078-4233
623-825-7317
http://www.asa-training.com
James Jarrett, Director

American Small Arms Academy
PO Box 12111
Prescott, AZ 86304
602-778-5623
Chuck Taylor, Instructor

Area 52 Smallarms Training Center
4809 Schley Road
Hillsborough, NC 27278
919-245-0013
area52training@cs.com

Argenbright International Training Institute
(law enforcement, military and corporate security)
4845 Old National Highway, Suite 210
Atlanta, Georgia 30337
800-235-4723

Arizona Defensive Firearms Training
PO Box 44302
Phoenix, Arizona 85064
602-279-3770
FAX: 602-279-0333
http://www.azccw.com
adft@azccw.com
Rick Barkett, Director

Arkansas Police Trainers
(law enforcement)
212 West Elm Street
Rogers, Arkansas 72756
501-621-1173 or 501-273-9270
FAX: 501-621-1131
Tim Keck, Executive Director

Auto Arms
738 Clearview
San Antonio, TX 78228
512-434-5450

AWARE
(Arming Women Against Rape and Endangerment)
PO Box 242
Bedford, MA 01730
781-893-0500

877-672-9273 Toll Free
http://www.aware.org

Bay Area Professionals for Firearms Safety & Education (Bayprofs)
1600 Saratoga Ave #403-181
San Jose, CA 95129
408-741-5218
(answering machine only)
http://www.bayprofs.org
Tom Laye, Training Director

Beretta Training
17601 Beretta Drive
Accokeek, MD 20607
301-283-2191
Russ Logan and Marcel James, Instructors

Blackheart International, LLC
112 Wood Street
Philippi, WV 26416
304-457-1280
FAX: 304-457-1281
support@bhigear.com
http://www.bhigear.com

Bob's Tactical
122 Lafayette Road
Salisbury, MA 01952
978-465-5561

Brantly and Associates, Inc.
3001 W. 39th St.
Suite 10
Orlando, FL 32839
407-650-1771
FAX: 407-650-8333
jamesbrantly@cs.com
http://brantlyandassociates.com

BSR, Inc.
PO Box 190
Summit Point, WV 25446
304-725-6512
FAX: 304-728-7124
office@bsr-inc.com
http://www.bsrfirearms-training.com

Burton's Firearm Instruction
(for women only)
PO Box 6084
Lynnwood, WA 98036-0084
206-774-7940
Gale Burton, Instructor

Calibre Press
(law enforcement and military personnel training)
666 Dundee Road, Ste. 1607
Northbrook, IL 60062-2760
708-498-5680

California Security & Safety Institute
706 E. Arrow Hwy, #E
Covina, CA 91722
800-281-1330
Steven Hurd, Director

Canadian Academy of Practical Shooting
C.P. 312 Roxboro, Quebec H8Y 3K4
Canada
514-696-8591
FAX: 514-696-2348
http://www.caps-inc.com
Dave Young, Director

Canadian Firearms Training
Ottawa, Ontario

Canada
613-443-0749
http://www.FirearmsTraining.ca
Dave Bartlett, President

Chapman Academy of Practical Shooting
4350 Academy Road
Hallsville, MO 65255-9707
800-847-0588
573-696-5544
FAX: 573-696-2266
http://www.chapmanacademy.com
John Skaggs, Director

Chelsea Gun Club of New York City, Inc.
c/o West Side Range
20 W. 20th Street
New York, NY 10011
212-929-7287
James D. Surdo, Instructor

Cirillo's Tactical Handgun Training
1211 Venetian Way
Panama City, FL 32405
Jim Cirillo, Instructor

CivilShield
Los Gatos, CA
408-354-1424
FAX: 408-399-2270
http://www.civilshield.com

Colorado Firearms Academy
20 S. Potomac Street
Aurora, Colorado 80012
303-360-5400
John Noble and Michael Schaffer, Instructors

Colorado Gun Training
2767 S. Parker Road, #253
Aurora, Colorado 80014
720-435-9964
Rick Vizachero, Director
train@theRange.com
http://firearmstrainingsite.com

Colorado Weapons Training
PO Box 745504
Arvada, Colorado 80006-5504
303-421-8541
http://ColoradoWeaponsTraining.com

Combative Concepts
826 Orange Avenue, #518
Coronado, CA 92118
619-521-2855

COMTAC, Ltd.
PO Box 12269
Silver Spring, MD 20908
301-924-4315
FAX: 301-924-3854
comtac@comtac.com
http://www.comtac.com
Charles A. Davis, Director of Training

Continental Threat Management
507 Owen Drive
Fayetteville, NC 28304
910-485-8805
NCLFI@aol.com
Timothy A. Noe, Director

Cumberland Tactics
PO Box 1400
Goodlettsville, TN 37070
615-822-7779
Randy@guntactics.com
http://www.guntactics.com/
Randy Cain, Director

Dalton's International Shootists Institute

PO Box 88
Acton, CA 93510
http://www.isishootists.com
Mike Dalton, Instructor

Dan Mitchell's Clay Target and Wing Shooting School

304 Roosevelt
Nampa, ID 83651
208-467-2793
http://www.idfishnhunt.com/
mitchell.htm

Defense Arts of Texas

214 N. 16th Suite B-6
McAllen, TX
Robert E. Henry, Director
956-682-0388

Defense Associates

PO Box 824
Fairfield, CT 06430
http://www.defenseassociates.com
203-261-8719

Defensive Firearms Academy

PO Box 615
Iselin, New Jersey 08830
http://www.dfatactics.com
Larry Mraz, Director
732-283-3314

Defensive Firearms Consultants

PO Box 27431
Towson, MD 21285
410-321-6522

Defensive Solutions

190 Cedar Circle
Powell, TN 37849
865-945-5612
info@defensivesolutions.com
http://www.defensivesolutions.com

Defensive Training for the Armed Citizen

(DEFTAC)
5712 Folkstone Lane
Orlando, FL 32822
407-208-0751
deftac03@aol.com
http://members.aol.com/deftac03
Jon A. Custis, Instructor

Defense Training International, Inc.

749 S. Lemay Ste. A3-337
Ft.Collins, Colorado 80301
970-482-2520
FAX: 970-482-0548
dti@frii.com
http://www.defense-training.com
John S. Farnam, President

Defensive Use of Firearms

PO Box 4227
Show Low, AZ 85902-4227
http://www.spw-duf.info

Denton County Sports Association, Inc.

409 Copper Canyon Road
Denton County, TX 76226
940-241-2376
dcsa@airmail.net
http://www.dentoncountysports.com
Lonnie Ward, Director

DTOM Enterprises
PO Box 415
Bloomingdale, MI 49026-0415
616-628-5039
http://DTOM.us
MTS@DTOM.us

Executive Security Services International
Box 5585
Huntsville, Ontario, Canada P1H 2L5
705-788-1957
http://www.essi.cjb.net

Farris Firearms Training
102 Jeremiah Court
Rockvale, Tennessee 37153
615-907-4892
http://www.farrisfirearms.com
training@farrisfirearms.com

Federal Law Enforcement Training Center
(FLETC)
(law enforcement training)
Glynco, GA 31524
800-743-5382
FAX: 912-267-3144
Gerald Brooks, Program Specialist

Firearms Academy of Redding
1530 Market Street
Redding, CA 96001
916-244-2190

Firearms Academy of Seattle
PO Box 400
Onalaska, WA 98570
360-978-6100
FAX: 360-978-6102

http://www.firearmsacademy.com
Marty Hayes, Instructor

Firearms International Training Academy
5139 Stanart Street
Norfolk, VA 23502
757-461-9153
FAX: 757-461-9155
Gerry Fockler, Director

Firearms Research & Instruction, Inc.
PO Box 732
Abingdon, MD 21009
877-456-5075
http://www.f-r-i.com
steves02@gte.net
Steven Silverman, President

Firearms Training Associates
PO Box 554
Yorba Linda, CA 92885-0554
714-701-9918
FAX: 714-777-9318
Bill Murphy, Instructor
http://www.ftatv.com

Firearm Training Center
The Bullet Hole Range
78 Rutgers St
Belleville, NJ 07109
201-919-0414
Anthony P. Colandro, Director
http://www.FirearmTrainingCenter.com

Firearms Training Center
9555 Blandville Road
West Paducah, KY 42086
502-554-5886

Firearms Training Institute

1044 Desert View Dr
Twin Falls, ID 83301
208-735-1469
scoobys@cyberhighway.net

Firearmz - Firearms Training and Defense

PO Box 344
Temple, Georgia 30179-0344
770-562-8663
http://www.firearmz.net

Front Sight Firearms Training Institute

PO Box 2619
Aptos, CA 95001
800-987-7719
FAX: 831-684-2137
http://www.frontsight.com
info@frontsight.com
Dr. Ignatius Piazza, Director

Global Security Complex

5750 Herring Road
Arvin, CA 93203
805-845-7011
FAX: 805-845-7945
global@lightspeed.net

Glock, Inc.

(law enforcement and military personnel training)
PO Box 369
Smyrna, GA 30081
404-432-1202
Al Bell, Director of Training
Frank DiNuzzo, Assistant Director of Training

Guardian Group International

21 Warren Street, Suite 3E
New York, NY 10007
212-619-2828

Gunner Joe's Bullseye Academy

12247 Buckskin Trail
Poway, CA 92964-6005
858-486-6201
Joe Vaineharrison, Instructor

GunSafety - TampaBay

PO Box 26393
Tampa, Florida 33623-6393
813-354-2799
Michael Perry, Owner
http://www.gunsafetytampa.com

Gunsite Academy, Inc.

2900 West Gunsite Road
Pauldin, AZ 86334-4301
520-636-4565
FAX: 520-636-1236
Buz Mills, Owner
http://www.gunsite.net

Guntek Firearms Training

4400 A Ambassador Caffery Parkway #310
Lafayette, LA 70508
337-984-8711
FAX: 337-993-1159
identify@bellsouth.net

Halo Group, The

316 California Ave
Suite 748
Reno, NV 89509
888-255-HALO
training@thehalogroup.com

Handgun Instruction
Fresno, CA
209-442-8102 or 209-221-9415
Laurie Anderson and Ken Zachary,
Instructors

Heckler & Koch, Inc.
International Training Division
(law enforcement and military
personnel training)
21480 Pacific Boulevard
Sterling, VA 20166-8903
703-450-1900
FAX: 703-450-8180
John Meyer, Jr., Director

HomeSafe Protective Training
5100 Burchette Rd., #3403
Tampa, FL 33647
813-979-7119 Beeper: 813-673-7016
Bret Bartlett, Director

Illinois Small Arms Institute
3512 Roxford Drive
Champaign, IL 61821
217-356-0704
John W. Bowman, Director

Insight Firearms Training Development
PO Box 12293
Prescott, Arizona 86304-2293
8662NSIGHT
FAX: 928-776-4668
http://www.insightfirearmstraining.com

InSights Training Center, Inc.
PO Box 3585
Bellevue, WA 98009
425-739-0133
http://www.insightstraining.com
Greg Hamilton, Instructor

Institute of Security Services
(tactical response team training)
1205 Banner Hill Rd.
Erwin, TN 37650-9301
800-441-0081
FAX: 615-743-2361

International Academy of Tactical Training Systems
#8 129 2nd Ave. N
Saskatoon, Saskatchewan
Canada S7K 2A9
306-975-1995
Brad Hutchinson, Director
http://www.attscanada.com
ntc@sk.sympatico.ca

International Association of Law Enforcement Firearms Instructors, Inc. IALEFI
25 Country Club Road, Suite 707
Gilford, NH 03246
603-524-8787
FAX: 603-524-8856
Robert D. Bossey, Executive Director
ialefi@lr.net
http://www.ialefi.com

International Rescue and Tactical Consultants (I.R.T.C.)
(law enforcement and private
security training)
PO Box 1128
Westhampton Beach, NY 11978
516-288-0414
Walter Britton & Gary Gross, Instructors

International Tactical Training Seminars Inc.
11718 Barrington Court, #506
Los Angeles, CA 90049
310-471-2029
http://www.intltactical.com
Brett McQueen, Instructor

ISI (Instinctive Shooting International)
(law enforcement, military, qualified civilians)
PO Box 6528
Houston, TX 77265-6528
713-666-0269
FAX: 713-666-9791
isi@wt.net
Hanan Yadin, Head Instructor

James A. Neal Public Safety Training Center (law enforcement)
PO Box 579
Toccoa, Georgia 30577
706-282-7012
http://www.jamesanealtraining.com

Ladies Handgun Clinics
2631 New Hope Church Road
Raleigh, NC 27604
919-872-8499

Lane Community College
4000 East 30th Ave.
Eugene, OR 97405-0092
503-726-2252
FAX: 503-726-3958
Michael Steen, Instructor

Law Enforcement Educators
789 F.M. 1637

Valley Mills, Texas 76689
800-527-2403
Carl C. Chandler, Jr., Instructor
http://www.carlchandler.com

Lethal Force Institute (LFI)
PO Box 122
Concord, NH 03302-0122
603-224-6814
http://www.ayoob.com
Massad Ayoob, Director

Loss Prevention Services of New Jersey
PO Box 15
Mt. Arlington, NJ 07856
973-347-2002
FAX: 973-347-2321
lpsofnjinc@webtv.com

Malins Defense Systems
2642 W.
Javelina Ave., Suite 207
Mesa, AZ 85202
602-838-8139
defense_systmems@hotmail.com
Darrell Malin, Instructor

Marksman's Enterprise
PO Box 556
Stevensville, Montana 59870
406-777-3557
crews@sprynet.com Jim Crews, Instructor

Marksmanship Training Group, Inc.
2549 W. Golf Rd. #217
Hoffman Estates, IL 60194
630-205-1369
http://www.kapnick.net/mtg.html
Brian Kapnick, Primary Instructor

Martial Arts Resource
PO Box 110841
Campbell, CA 95011-0841
408-866-5127
http://MartialArtsResource.com
Ray Terry, Head Instructor

Massachusetts Firearms Seminars
PO Box 881
Lee, MA 01238
413-243-2195
http://www.mafseminars.com

Midwest Tactical Training Institute
11311 S. Skunk Hollow Road
Mt. Carroll, IL 61053
815-244-2815
Andrew Casavant, Instructor

Midwest Training Group, Inc.
1514 Cortland Drive
Naperville, IL 60565
630-579-0351
andykemp@msn.com
Andy Kemp, Director

Mid-Atlantic Training Resources
112 North Wood Street
Philippi, WV 26416
(304) 457-1280
http://www.ma-tr.com/

Mid-South Institute of Self-Defense
(law enforcement and military personnel training)
5582 Blythe Road
Lake Cornorant, MS 38641

http://www.weaponstraining.com
John Shaw, Instructor

MINDRICK Security Academy and Shooting School
Budd Road Box 747
Phillipsport, NY 12769
914-647-4048
http://www.mindrick.com
Fredrick Vobis, Director

Modern Warrior Defensive Tactics Institute
(law enforcement training)
711 N. Wellwood Ave.
Lindenhurst, NY 11757
800-33-WARRIOR
FAX: 516-226-5454
George Demetriou

National Law Enforcement Training Center
4948 Westwood Road
Kansas City, MO 64112
800-445-0857
FAX: 816-531-3416
http://www.odinpress.com

National Rifle Association
11250 Waples Mill Road
Fairfax, VA 22030
800-672-3888
http://www.nra.org

Northeast Training Institute
130 N. Fifth Street, Suite 804
Reading, PA 19601
215-872-3433

NOR-CAL Training Academy

2016 Oakdale Ave.
San Francisco, CA 94124-2098
415-550-8282
Bob Borissoff, Instructor

Oceanside Shooting Academy

618 Airport Road
Oceanside, CA
760-945-8567
Bill Jorgensen, Instructor

OffShoots Training Institute

(law enforcement and military
personnel training)
119 Cotillion
San Antonio, Texas 78213
210-541-9884
FAX: 210-541-9884
www.offshootstraining.com
Jerry Lane, Instructor

Operational Support Services, Inc.

19018 Candleview Drive
Spring, TX 77388
281-288-9190 x205
FAX: 281-288-7019
opsupp@getus.com
David Lee Salmon II, Law
Enforcement
Training Director

Options for Personal Security

PO Box 489
Sebring, FL 33871-0489
877-636-4677
http://www.optionsforpersonal
security.com
Andy Stanford, Director

Oregon Firearms Academy

Brownsville, OR
541-451-5532
http://oregonfirearms.d2g.com

Peregrine Corporation, The

PO Box 170
Bowers, PA 19511
610-682-7147
FAX: 610-682-7158
Emanuel Kapelsohn, President

Personal Defense Institute

2603 NW 13th St., #205
Gainesville, FL 32609
904-378-6425
afn01182@afn.org
Jeff Dissell and W.L. Fisher, Instructors

Personal Defense Training

5220 Linnadine Way
Norcross, GA 30092
404-403-5739
david@personaldefensetraining.com
http://www.personaldefense
training.com
David Blinder, Director

Personal Protection Concepts

PO Box 340485
Dayton, Ohio 45434
937-371-7816
info@ppctraining.com
http://www.ppctraining.com
Brady Smith, Instructor

Personal Protection Strategies

(specializing in women's training)
9903 Santa Monica Blvd., Suite 300
Beverly Hills, CA 90212
310-281-1762
Paxton Quigley, Instructor

Personal Protection Training

PO Box 2008
Woodland Park, Colorado
719-687-8226
southeops@hotmail.com
A.C. Bowolick, Instructor

Personal Responsibility, Inc

221 Fourth Avenue North
Second Floor
Nashville, TN 37219
615-242-3348
FAX: 615-242-6502
John M.L. Brown, President

Personal Safety Institute

15 Central Way, Suite 319
Kirkland, WA 98033
206-827-2015
Ginny Lyford, Director

Personal Security Consulting

PO Box 8118
Albuquerque, NM 87198-8118
505-255-8610

Personal Security & Safety Training (PSST)

PO Box 381
Eagle, ID 83616
208-939-8051
Bruce and Nancy Priddy, Instructors

Police Training Institute

(law enforcement only)
University of Illinois
1004 S. 4th St.
Champaign, IL 61820
217-333-7811
John W. Bowman, Instructor

Police Training Division

(law enforcement and military
personnel training)
2 Edgebrook Lane
Monsey, NY 10952
Peter Tarley, Instructor

Plus P Technology, Inc.

Minneapolis, MN
612-660-4263
plusp@plusp.com
http://www.plusp.com/

Practical Firearms Training

Covington, VA
540-559-3074
FAX: 540-559-4151
pgpft@cfw.com

Practical Shooting Academy, The

PO Box 630
Olathe, Colorado 81425
970-323-6111
http://www.practicalshootingacad.
com
Ron Avery, Instructor

PRO

3953 Indianola Ave
Columbus, OH 43214
614-263-1601
http://www.peoplesrights.org

Progressive F.O.R.C.E. Concepts

PO Box 336301
N. Las Vegas, NV 89033
702-647-1126
FAX: 702-647-7325
http://www.PFCtraining.com
Steve Krystek, Director

ProTac Glocal Inc

PMB 233
1208 E. Bethany Dr. Suite 2
Allen, Texas 75002
972-359-0303
http://www.protacglobal.com
Chris Grollnek, President

Pro-Tek

5154 Cemetery Road
Bainbridge, NY 13733
607-343-9999
Tim Roberts, Chief Instructor
tactical@mkl.com

R & S Protection Services

4401 N. Dogwood Dr.
Kenai, Alaska 99611
907-283-7001
Raymond Carr, Instructor
alaskaknives@alaskaknives.com
http://www.alaskaknives.com

Remington Shooting School

Remington Arms Company
14 Hoefler Avenue
Ilion, NY 13357
315-895-3574
Dale P. Christie, Director

Rocky Mountain Combat Applications Training

PO Box 535
Lake George, Colorado 80827
FAX: 719-748-8557
http://www.rmcat.com

Rocky Mountain Gun Safety

3812 E. Pikes Peak Ave
Suites 207-208
Colorado Springs, Colorado 80916
719-638-7406
rockymountaingunsafety
@yahoo.com

Rogers Shooting School

1736 Saint Johns Bluff Rd.
Jacksonville, Florida 32246
904-613-1196
http://rogers-shooting-school.com

Rural/Urban Tactical Training

17660 N. 35th Street
Phoenix, AZ 85032
602-701-1614

Scott, McDougall & Associates

7950 Redwood Drive
Cotati, CA 94931
707-795-BANG
Mac Scott, Instructor

Security Awareness & Firearms Education

(SAFE)
PO Box 864
Post Falls, ID 83854-0864
http://SAFE-LLC.com
staysafe@SAFE-LLC.com

208-773-3624
Robert B. Smith, Director

Security Training International

PO Box 492
Vista, CA 92085
760-940-6385
Candace Crawford, Instructor

Self Defense Firearms Training

5375 Industrial Drive, Suite 107
Huntington Beach, CA 92649-1545
Greg@firearmstraining.com
714-893-8676
FAX: 714-894-7656
Greg Block

Serious Sportsman, Inc.

100 Middletown Road
Pearl River, NY
914-735-7722
John Perkins, Instructor

Shawnee Hunt Club

PO Box 10531
Blacksburg, VA 24062
http://civic.bev.net/shawnee
Betty Strauss, Training Coordinator

Shoot-N-Iron, Inc.

17205 Gaddy Road
Shawnee, OK 74801
si-gun@swbell.net
http://www.shoot-n-iron.com
405-273-4822
FAX: 405-273-4180
Paul Abel, Instructor

Shooters-Edge

PO Box 3821

Beverly Hills, CA 90212
info@shooters-edge.com
http://www.shooters-edge.com
Bruce Krell, Instructor

Shootrite Firearms Academy

PO Box 189
Owens Cross Roads
Huntsville, AL 35763
http://www.shootrite.org
256-721-4602
Ed Aldrich & James McKee,
Instructors

Sierra Firearms Academy

PO Box 9640
Reno, NV 89507
mike@sierrafirearms.com
http://www.sierrafirearms.com
702-425-1678
Dave Keller and Mike Robbins,
Instructors

Sierra Firearms Training

2936 South West Street
Visalia, CA 93277
559-734-6150
559-280-5600 (cell)
Edward F. Peterson, Instructor

SIGARMS Academy

233 Exeter Road
Epping, NH 03042
http://www.sigarmsacademy.com
603-679-2003
Tim Connell, Director

Smith & Wesson Academy & Armorers School

2100 Roosevelt Avenue
Springfield, MA 01102-2208

800-331-0852 extension 255/265
Robert E. Hunt, Director

Southern Police Institute
(law enforcement training)
University of Louisville
Louisville, KY 40292
502-852-6561

South West Association of Trainers and COMSAT
PO Box 51510
Amarillo, Texas 79159
http://www.traintosurvive.com
806-874-1265
FAX: 806-874-1266
Jerry Holland, Director

Southwest Defensive Shooting Institute, L.L.C.
PO Box 190179-266
Dallas, Texas 75219
214-599-0309
A.W. McBee, Instructor

Southwest Tactical
4351 Sepulveda Blvd., Suite 450
Culver City, CA 90230
310-838-1275

Spartan Group LLC
PO Box 671
Mamers, NC 27552
877-9SPARTA
http://www.spartangroup.com

Specialized Training Associates
(NRA Training Counselor Workshops
and NRA Instructor Certification)
1313 N. Ritchie Ct. Suite 2100
Chicago, IL 60610

312-482-9910
FAX: 312-482-9960
PO Box 453
San Jose, CA 95052
408-985-1311
FAX: 408-985-1311
Lpyle@PaulRevere.org
Leroy Pyle, Director

Specter Tactical
60 River Road
East Haddam, Connecticut 06423-1460
860-526-5528
http://www.spectertactical.com
Chris Adams, Director

St. James Academy, The
PO Box 700
Birmingham, MI 48012
810-545-9000
Michael St. James, Instructor

Storm Mountain Training Center
Rt. 1 Box 60
Elk Garden, WV 26717
304-446-5526
http://www.stormmountain.com

Strategic Weapons Academy of Texas
100 N. MacArthur, Suite 120
Irving, TX 75061
972-256-3969
http://www.weaponsacademy.com
Tim Bulot, Executive Director

Sturm, Ruger & Company
(Law Enforcement Division)
Lacey Place
Southport, CT 06490
203-259-7843

Suarez International
2517 Sycamore Drive, #352
Simi Valley, CA 93065
805-582-2499 (Office and Fax)
Gabriel Suarez, President
http://www.gabesuarez.com

Surgical Shooting Inc.
13955 Stowe Drive
Poway, CA 92064
858-668-3453
FAX: 858-668-3457
Gary A. Lakis, COO
http://www.surgicalshooting.com

Tac One
PO Box 3215
Idaho Springs, Colorado 80452
303-698-4566
FAX: 303-582-3655
tacone@juno.com
Gary Cunningham, President

TACFIRE
(Tactical Firearms Training Institute)
2426 East Main St.
Ventura, CA 93003
805-652-1345
http://www.tacfire.com
Dave Manning, Chief Instructor

Tactical Defense Institute
2174 Bethany Ridge Road
West Union, OH 45693
937-544-7228
http://www.tdiohio.com

Tactical Defense International
5 Rose Lane
Apalachin, NY 13732
607-625-4488

glhblh@sg23.com
Gary Hellmers, Master Instructor

Tactical Edge
Security Consultants
19015 Parthenia Street, Suite 203
Northridge, CA 91324
818-890-3930

Tactical Firearms Training Team
16836 Algonquin St, Suite 120
Huntington Beach, CA 92649
714-846-8065
director@tftt.com
http://www.tftt.com
Max Joseph, Training Director

Tactical Force Institute
4231 Kodiak
Casper, WY 82604
307-266-1063
FAX: 307-472-5797
tfi0397@aol.com
Michael J. Wallace, Instructor

Tactical Gun
P.O. Box 51404
Phoenix, AZ 85048
480-706-8010

Tactical Handgun Training
PO Box 1817
Kingston, NY 12401
845-339-3440
FAX: 845-339-3451
http://www.tacticalhandguntraining.com
Ken Cooper, President

Tactical Shooting Academy
7366 Colonial Trail East

Surry, VA 23883
757-357-9881
http://www.tacticalshooting.com

Talon Enterprises
4 Locust Ave
Exeter, NH
603-772-7981
talon@ultranet.com
Bill Burroughs, Instructor

Talons Firearms Training, Inc.
11645 North Highway 287
LaPorte, Colorado 80535
303-493-2221
Ron Phillips and Kyle Caffey, Instructors

Team One Network
Law Enforcement Training Only
620 Richards Ferry Road
Fredericksburg, Virginia 22406
540-752-8190
FAX: 540-752-8192

Team Virginia
PO Box 1361
Chesterfield, VA 23832
804-931-4554
http://teamvirginia.tripod.com
Glenn Blandford, Instructor

Texas Small Arms Academy
Houston, TX
713-561-5335
Tim Oxley, Instructor

The Competitive Edge
(TCE)
PO Box 805
Oakville, Ontario

Canada L6J 5C5
905-849-6960
Nick Alexakos, Instructor

Threat Management Institute (TMI)
800 West Napa St.
Sonoma, CA 95476
707-939-0303
FAX: 707-939-8684
tmi@crl.com
Peter Kasler and Peggi Bird, Instructors

Thunder Ranch, Inc.
96747 Hwy 140 E.
Lakeview, OR 97630
541-947-4104
FAX: 541-947-4105
http://www.ThunderRanchInc.com
Clint Smith, Director

Top Gun Training Centre
1042 N. Mountain Ave. #B
PMB 303
Upland, CA 91786
800-677-4407
FAX: 888-677-4407
http://www.1topgun1.com
R.J. Kirschner, Director of Operations

Trident Concepts Research Group
PO Box 11955
Prescott, AZ 86304-1955
928-776-5326
FAX: 928-443-0174
http://www.tridentconcepts.com
Jeff Gonzales, Instructor

Trigger Time
185 Atkins lane

Carthage, NC 28327
(910) 947-1730
http://www.trigger-time.com/

Tugs 'n' Thugs Defensive Training

(specializing in, but not limited to, women's training)
16818 N. 56th St, #220
Scottsdale, AZ 85254
602-788-3609
KateAlex@aol.com

Turnipseed Stance

610 N. Alma School Road, #18-213
Chandler, AZ 85224
602-802-0346
http://www.turnipseedstance.com
Kent Turnipseed, Instructor

Universal Shooting Academy

4300 Highway 630 East
Frostpoint, FL 33843
305-688-0262
Frank Garcia, Director

Vital Options Institute

503 Trowbridge Street
Allegan MI 49010
616-686-1321
gbadams@datawise.net
Greg Adams and James Bay, Instructors

Wallin Video Productions

Deadly Force Division Videos
950 Highway 10 Northeast, Suite 110

Minneapolis, MN 55432
612-786-1486
Shelly Mydra

Weigand Shooting Seminars

685 South Main Road
Mountaintop, PA 18707
http://www.learntoshootpistol.com
Jack Weigand, Instructor

Whitten Arms

2770 Whitten Road
Memphis, TN 38133
901-386-7002
Jim Littlejohn, Director

Williams Associates Protective Services, LLC.

74 Olivia St., Box 164
Derby, CT 06418
203-924-1784
FAX: 203-924-1784
http://www.wa-protective.com
Brian S. Williams, President

Wicklander-Zulawski & Associates

(law enforcement training)
555 E. Butterfield Rd. Ste. 302
Lombard, IL
800-222-7789

Yavapai Firearms Academy

PO Box 27290
Prescott Valley, AZ 86312
520-772-8262
http://www.yfainc.com
Louis Awerbuck, Instructor

APPENDIX B

PROGRESS WORKSHEETS

This Appendix was added for you to track your progress with certain drills, allowing you to focus more on what you have to practice and less on skills you perform well. Be honest with your results so you can have a truthful assessment of your ability and progress. You can determine the number of rounds and type of targets on some of these charts or re-designate them for your needs.

ONE-SHOT DRAW

Date	Distance	Time

SPEED RELOAD

Date	Distance	Time

PRESENTATION FROM POSITION 3 TO 4

Date	Distance	Time

DOUBLE TAP

Date	Distance	Time

180-DEGREE PIVOT

Date	Distance	Time

FAILURE-TO-EJECT MALFUNCTION

Date	Distance	Time

SHOOTER'S CHOICE_____

Date	Distance	Time
_____	_____	_____
_____	_____	_____
_____	_____	_____
_____	_____	_____

SIX-SHOT RHYTHM DRILL

Date / Distance		Shot Time	Split Times
_____	1	_____	_____
_____	2	_____	_____
_____	3	_____	_____
_____	4	_____	_____
_____	5	_____	_____
	6		
_____	1	_____	_____
_____	2	_____	_____
_____	3	_____	_____
_____	4	_____	_____
_____	5	_____	_____
_____	6	_____	_____
_____	1	_____	_____
_____	2	_____	_____
_____	3	_____	_____
_____	4	_____	_____
_____	5	_____	_____
_____	6	_____	_____

Ten Simple Rules
Of Life As A Gun Fighter

1. Bring a gun. Preferably, bring at least two.

2. Anything worth shooting is worth shooting twice.

3. Only hits count.

4. If your shooting stance is good you're probably not moving   fast enough or using cover correctly.

5. Keep shooting until the threat no longer exists.

6. If you can choose what to bring to a gun fight, bring a long gun and a friend.

7. In ten years nobody will remember the details of caliber, stance, or tactics. They will only remember who lived.

8. If you are not shooting you should be reloading or running.

9. Accuracy is relative: most combat shooting standards will be more dependent on "pucker factor" than the inherent accuracy of the gun.

10. Someday someone may kill you with your own gun, but they should have to beat you to death with it because it is empty.

Author Unknown